The Colour of Distance

The
of

New Zealand writers in France

edited by Jenny Bornholdt

Colour Distance

French writers in New Zealand

& Gregory O'Brien

Victoria University Press

VICTORIA UNIVERSITY PRESS
Victoria University of Wellington
PO Box 600 Wellington
http://www.vuw.ac.nz/vup

First published 2005

National Library of New Zealand Cataloguing-in-Publication Data

The colour of distance : New Zealand writers in France,
French writers in New Zealand / edited by Jenny Bornholdt and
Gregory O'Brien.
ISBN 0-86473-505-7
1. New Zealand literature. 2. French literature—Translations into
English. 3. New Zealand—Literary collections.
4. France—Literary collections. I. Bornholdt, Jenny, 1960-
II. O'Brien, Gregory, 1961-
NZ820.8—dc 22

Published with the generous support of the French Embassy, Wellington,
to mark the sixtieth anniversary of diplomatic relations between
New Zealand and France

Published with the assistance of grants from
The Katherine Mansfield Trust
and Creative New Zealand

Printed by PrintLink, Wellington

Contents

Preface

Why an anthology of literary texts to mark the sixtieth anniversary of diplomatic relations between New Zealand and France? Literature isn't ordinarily a sphere of official exchange.

One of the reasons is that literature shapes our imagination. As a teenager, my first vision of New Zealand was fed by Jules Verne's *Captain Grant's Children*. For a young Frenchman, New Zealand is the kiwi discovered by Robert, it's Paganel in Maori dress, it's the geysers and volcanoes of Taupo and the Terraces.

For adults, it is invariably literature, sometimes under the guise of other artistic vehicles, notably film, that arouses their curiosity. The work of Jane Mander and even Janet Frame was revealed to many in France through the films of Jane Campion. The moment that *Whale Rider* was projected onto French screens, readers had access to the first French translation of Witi Ihimaera's work.

Literature also alters our perception of reality. Any French person who walks along the sands of Hokitika, or any other corner of New Zealand, can in no way avoid being struck by the sheer beauty of this land. But if he has read Keri Hulme, or Nadine Ribault, his view shifts and thereafter he sees the landscape across the text.

And lastly, literature pulses with unexpected inter-connections. When I was living in Montmartre, I read Francis Carco, renowned for his writing on Paris in the 1930s, and *Jésus la Caille* became one of my bedside books. What a surprise to rediscover him in another book, *Les Innocents*, inspired by his relationship with Katherine Mansfield! What a discovery to find in this anthology a piece by Blaise Cendrars directly influenced by New Zealand!

New Zealand writers have a unique and long-standing relationship with France, thanks to the Meridian Energy Katherine Mansfield Memorial Fellowship residency in Menton. Over the last few years it has found its counterpart thanks to the Randell Cottage Writers Trust residency in Wellington. This anthology bears witness to the elective affinities between writers from these two countries. Its realisation would not have been possible without the work of the two editors, the commitment of Victoria University Press and the support of the Katherine Mansfield Trust. May they be hereby recognised for their accomplishment.

Jean-Michel Marlaud
French Ambassador to New Zealand

Introduction

The Day/Night Shift
Writers and artists in transit

If the project of colonialism necessarily involves the shipping off of citizens to the far reaches of the earth, the imaginative project—of which the writing in this book is a part—has, over the past century, tended to work the other way around. A far greater number of New Zealand writers and artists have washed up on the shores of France than French writers and artists have made the trip to New Zealand.

A timeline noting earlier artistic encounters between France and New Zealand would, however, highlight considerable activity in the South Seas during the nineteenth century, when the engraver Charles Meryon spent a tour of duty at Akaroa and painter Paul Gauguin stopped over in Auckland. By the early 20th century, traffic was moving in the opposite direction: Katherine Mansfield was convalescing on the Côte d'Azur and, two years later, Frances Hodgkins's easel was embedded in the good soil of St Paul du Var.

Since the colonial period, writers and artists moving between the two countries have been part of a discontinuous narrative, a sequence of isolated moments rather than a constant stream of orderly or organised interaction: An infantryman returns to New Zealand after World War Two, bringing with him a love of modern painting. A young poet goes hunting for Matisse paintings in the museums of Europe. A French philosopher smokes a pipe on a west coast beach, not far from Auckland . . . Expanding the terms of this intriguing, if at times surreal, history of cultural coming and going we also note the Franco-Romanian poet Tristan Tzara reciting traditional Maori 'sound-poems' at the Cabaret Voltaire in 1917, and record Henri Matisse sailing towards Tahiti in 1930 on a boat manned entirely—and much to his displeasure—by monolingual New Zealanders.

In recent decades the pattern of interaction has become more complex and livelier thanks to the increase in international travel. Since it was first offered in 1970, the Katherine Mansfield Memorial Fellowship has established a literary continuum, with one New Zealand writer per annum shipping out to Menton on the Mediterranean coast. Since 2002, the Randell Cottage Fellowship in Wellington has effected some reciprocal traffic, bringing Nadine Ribault, Charles Juliet and, most recently, Pierre Furlan here. With both fellowships, at the time of writing, active and well-supported, the future of this ongoing literary dialogue appears secure.

The creative work in this anthology was produced during the period 1945–2005—aside from the inclusion of work by Katherine Mansfield, who is an inescapable presence and ongoing force in the literary traditions of both New Zealand and France. (M. K. Joseph's poems referring to events in 1944 are from his 1950 collection *Imaginary Islands*. Blaise Cendrars's memoir of visiting New Zealand in the 1920s was written three decades later.) Zealous readers are urged to seek out earlier accounts of Franco-New Zealand relations in the writing of Jules Verne—whose 1868 novel *Les enfants du Capitaine Grant* includes a shipwreck on the New Zealand coast and capture of the book's main characters by a tribe of cannibalistic Maori—and the proto-surrealistic engravings of Charles Meryon, about whom Vincent O'Sullivan writes in this book. This selection does not attempt to cover the entire range of Franco-New Zealand writing, which would also include much travel journalism, sports commentary, cookbooks, memoirs and the ramblings of many a wine-drinker. Rather, we have set out to capture a few imaginative currents, sparks that have flown.

While the two countries have never had to share the burden of the colonial power–colony relationship which characterised New Zealand's interactions with Great Britain, they have had their ups and downs. New Zealand involvement in two world wars established grounds for an enduring friendship, the only real threat to which has been disagreement over nuclear testing in the Pacific region—a tension brought to a head by the *Rainbow Warrior* affair in 1985.

Dominant among the various forms of Franco-New
Zealand cultural interaction, the game of rugby now appears
to provide a kind of baseline for the ongoing relationship
between the two nations. (Bill Manhire's snapshots taken in
the small French town of Alzon—see pages 87 and 88—are a
mild-mannered manifestation of this.) Further advancing this
tradition, the 2003 Randell Cottage Fellow, Charles Juliet—
accompanied by his wife M. L.—was sighted on more than
one occasion braving the fierce Wellington elements to attend
matches at the Westpac Stadium, a handy distance from the
cottage. Rugby writing is represented in this collection by
excerpts from Denis Lalanne's *La Mêlée Fantastique* (1962) and
Lloyd Jones's *The Book of Fame* (2000).

Visitors from the opposite side of the world tend to find
much to embrace and usually a few things to complain about
in their host country. Such are the inclinations of travellers
in any direction. Mansfield's complaints about the French
have been often quoted, but a love of southern France also
permeates her writings. In New Zealand literary history,
Mansfield remains a persistent ghost, adopting all manner
of guises: passionate traveller, wild colonial girl, delicate
flower, tragic figure . . . Her afterlife is acknowledged in this
book not only by her own writing but in the contributions of
C. K. Stead, Fleur Adcock, Riemke Ensing, Witi Ihimaera
and Charles Juliet.

Mansfield's near-contemporary, the painter Frances
Hodgkins, was, like the writer, bipolar in her relationship with
France. She wrote from the Alpes Maritimes in April 1924:
'. . . how I welcome a chance of a trip to NZ where life is
less strenuous & overcrowded & bankrupt than this weary
demented old Europe—striving after peace & security but still
in a welter of unrest & misery . . .' Yet only a few days later
Hodgkins was gushing about the place: 'I have been living
at this darling abode of light & peace for nearly 3 weeks,
marvelling at my luck . . . I want to spend the Summer making
attractive best-selling pictures—such as flower markets & red
sails & blue Mediterranean . . . You will love my garden & the
sacred citron tree in the centre of the courtyard—heavy with
fruit—I eat my meals beneath its shade.'[1]

Dick Frizzell, *Apollinaire at 21 from an age when art seemed much more fun*, 1978. Oil on board, 610 x 412 mm, collection of Stewart Main (photograph by Michael Roth)

Writing *about* France has certainly played a part in New Zealand literature to date—not only in Mansfield's celebrated stories but also M. K. Joseph's 1976 novel *A Soldier's Tale* (which was filmed by Larry Parr in 1988, with Gabriel Byrne in the main role). C. K. Stead, as both poet and novelist, has often returned to France as subject over the past four decades. Elizabeth Knox's *The Vintner's Luck*, set in Burgundy, achieved international success (and was translated into French by Pierre Furlan in 2003). While most New Zealanders who have written about France have travelled there, the imaginative space the country occupies is often the primary one. It was a year after the publication of *The Vintner's Luck* that Knox spent four months in France. And while Stead spent many weeks walking the appropriate streets before writing *Paris* (1984), the illustrator of that book had never set foot in the city. Travelling to France often adds the finishing touches to one's idea of the place, rather than building it up from scratch. A tension between the 'real' and the 'imagined' France pervades many of the contributions in this book.[2] New Zealanders often first discover Paris through the paintings of Marc Chagall, the photographs of Henri Cartier-Bresson, the poems of Apollinaire and the music of Erik Satie. 'City so long announced come home to my dreams,' Stead's *Paris* begins, then proceeds:

> You have come a long journey to enter the bathroom of
>   Pierre Bonnard,
> to take to task Picasso in the light of a cubist dawn,
> to look through Matisse's windows at the palms of his hands
> as they're blown against the blue of a Mediterranean night.[3]

French art has captivated New Zealand poets, as it has painters, over the past six decades. Soon after returning from military service, M. K. Joseph wrote the sequence 'Painters' in homage to Georges Braque, Pablo Picasso, Georges Rouault and Henri Matisse, whose crisp, sonorous paintings he evoked:

> Blue sings round in the always
> o of the arched air over

> the square window over the coral town blue
> in the grey in the rose
> and amber of an always
> afternoon where music plays
> in the adjacent room . . .[4]

By the mid-1960s, Mallarmé and Rimbaud were being read avidly by an emerging generation of New Zealand writers, and the young Auckland-based poet Michael Jackson was busily translating Blaise Cendrars. The influence of French poetry—particularly the work of Jacques Prévert and Guillaume Apollinaire—is registered in the work of New Zealand poets such as Ian Wedde, C. K. Stead, Cilla McQueen and Riemke Ensing.

Gauguin in Auckland

Some decades before Colin McCahon, Toss Woollaston and Doris Lusk were discovering reproductions of Cézanne, Van Gogh, Picasso and Matisse, French modernism made an early appearance in New Zealand in the person of Paul Gauguin, who stopped over for ten days en route to Tahiti in 1895. Peter Bland adopts the guise of the painter in his poem 'Gauguin in Auckland', and details the circumstances of his stay:

> I'm stuck in a swamp called *Freemans Bay*.
> (The ship for Papeete will take ten days
> to repair a propellor blade. We ran
> into some whales.) My host
> is a mad Parisian who claims
> he invaded this place with a couple of brigs
> over fifty years ago . . .[5]

Gauguin's Auckland sojourn—he stayed at the Albert Hotel in Queen Street—proved not quite the waste of time he first thought at. A trip to the Auckland Museum gave rise to a number of still existent drawings of Maori carvings which the artist later incorporated into important paintings. A century later the influence of Maori design upon Gauguin's art has been the subject of scholarship by, amongst others, Bronwen Nicholson and Roger Neich.[6] Jonathan Mane-Wheoki has written that Gauguin's amalgam of traditional and Western modernist art—with all its attendant issues—foreshadowed the work of both Maori and Pakeha artists a century later.[7]

For the 1995 centenary of Gauguin's visit, curator John Perry organised a commemorative exhibition, 'Kiaora Paora; Paul Gauguin in Aotearoa/NZ', at RKS ART, Auckland. However, upon the French Government's announcement, shortly before the exhibition opened, of another round of nuclear testing at Mururoa Atoll, the project changed direction dramatically, and virtually every work exhibited engaged directly with the nuclear issue.[8]

The French in the South Pacific

In recent decades, a few French novelists have passed through New Zealand, among them Michel Butor and Alain Robbe-Grillet, who put in a languid performance at the 1986 Writers and Readers Week in Wellington. 'Serge Gainsbourg with a PhD', was how one audience member described the session. Around this time, literary theory, a lot of it French, was sweeping through academia in this country, for better or worse. If Robbe-Grillet appeared happily oblivious to any specifics of place, other French visitors as various as the nineteenth-century missionary Mother Suzanne Aubert (see Jessie Munro's 1996 biography) and the philosopher Jacques Derrida have engaged productively with local traditions, Maori and Pakeha.

Described by Jonathan Bywater as 'the original exponent of the notorious practice of deconstruction . . . his name . . . all but synonymous with the moment of "theory" in the arts', Derrida looks completely at home in a photograph taken at Karekare beach during his 1999 tour.[9] The image appeared on the cover of *Derrida Downunder*. The editors of that book, Laurence Simmons and Heather Worth, noted the extraordinary success of the philosopher's visit:

The Colour of Distance

Derrida Downunder
(Dunmore Press, 2001)

> There exists a generalised belief that New Zealanders,
> who see themselves as eminently pragmatic, exhibit a
> resistance to theory, and French theory in particular . . .
> The success of Derrida's visit to New Zealand, his sell-out
> public lecture in the Auckland Town Hall, and the fully
> subscribed conference dedicated to the relevance of his
> work in the Antipodes, is part of an increasing reversal of
> that resistance to theory . . .

Cultural traffic is most effective when it flows both ways.
While Derrida's visit was a euphoric experience for New
Zealand audiences and a great moment for the study of
philosophy in this country, Simmons and Worth noted that it
also made an impression on Derrida. In a book published the
following year—*Le Toucher, Jean-Luc Nancy*, an exploration of
the multiple forms of touching—the philosopher mused upon
his visit to New Zealand, specifically his experience of being
welcomed onto a marae and the Maori ritual of the hongi.[10]
Two years later, in March 2001, the philosopher/
photographer Jean Baudrillard received a similarly warm
reception in Auckland. The publication arising from that

tour—a companion volume to *Derrida Downunder*—was *Baudrillard West of the Dateline*, edited by Victoria Grace, Heather Worth and Laurence Simmons.

New Zealand birdsong in French music

Beyond the realms of literature and the visual arts, in recent decades New Zealand composers and musicians have been drawn to Paris. Frederick Page's memoir of meeting composer Pierre Boulez is included in this book. During 1964 and 1965, composer Jenny McLeod studied at the Paris Conservatoire, where she was taught by Olivier Messiaen.

Another New Zealander at the Conservatoire, Robin Maconie, was responsible for the incorporation of New Zealand birdsong into Messiaen's music. Arriving in the composer's class in 1963 and well aware of the role birdsong played in his music, Maconie gave Messiaen a boxed set of native birdsong recordings. The following year, Messiaen included transcriptions of tui and bellbirds in his *Couleurs de la Cité céleste*. Among the many songs that permeate his *Concert à quatre* (1990-91) are those of three New Zealand birds: blue-wattled crow, bush canary and kakapo. Maconie points out that, in Messiaen's compositions, birds always symbolise paradise—and, after 1964, New Zealand birds figured disproportionately large in his music.[11]

Jenny McLeod wrote that studying with Messiaen 'opened my ears, and completely changed my perception of music'. She told Sarah Shieff in a recent interview: 'Although [Messiaen] certainly taught me things about music, the most important lessons weren't to do with music at all—they were to do with life . . . I had never met a more charitable, kindly, humble, utterly transparent soul.'[12]

Continental drift, new wave

The French cinematic tradition remains an important reference point for New Zealand film-making, with the *nouvelle vague* film-makers who emerged during the 1960s a major

The Colour of Distance

'Le Corbusier',
1947, photogram
by Len Lye
(courtesy Len Lye
Foundation)

influence on subsequent New Zealand directors such as Tony
Williams (who worked for a time with Alain Resnais). In recent
years New Zealand cinema has drawn considerable audiences
in France—most notably Niki Caro's *Whale Rider* and Peter
Jackson's *Lord of the Rings* trilogy. Also notable in the French
context is the work of New Zealand-born kinetic sculptor
and film-maker Len Lye (1901–1980), who was the subject of
an exhibition and film programme at the Centre Pompidou
in 2000.[13] More recently Lye has featured in a major group
exhibition at the same institution, 'Sons et Lumières', which
explored the use of sound and light in avant-garde practice
through the 20th century. (Roger Horrocks points out that
kinetic art has always been best understood in Europe.[14] Not
surprisingly, two France-based artists, Jean Tinguely and
Nicholas Schöffer, can be considered among Lye's closest
creative allies.) In the 1930s Lye passed through Paris, where,
as Horrocks has noted, he attended the salon of Gertrude
Stein and designed covers for Nancy Cunard's Hours Press.
In 1947 he made a photogram of the Swiss-French architect
Le Corbusier in the surrealist style. Posthumously, Lye

continues to have a colourful career in France. Programmed by MTV Europe (who sponsored the 2000 Centre Pompidou exhibition), his experimental films are finding a new audience among the young and hip.

The Centre Pompidou was the site of an important New Zealand art commission in 1989 when an aerial sculpture by Christchurch-based Neil Dawson was featured in the exhibition of international art, 'Magiciens de la Terre'. The 4.5-metre in diameter, steel globe-shape was suspended outside the gallery to the wonderment of pedestrians and gallery visitors alike.

A key figure in introducing French modernism to New Zealand, Louise Henderson (née Sauze) was born in Paris in 1902 and raised in an artistic milieu. Her father was, for a time, secretary to Auguste Rodin. She married and emigrated to New Zealand in 1925, remaining here until her death in 1994, apart from a further year of study in France in 1952. Just as it had for earlier painters such as Frances Hodgkins, Owen Merton, Raymond McIntyre and John Weeks, France served as a finishing school for many of the important emerging New Zealand artists of the 1960s, among them Don Peebles, Pat Hanly, John Drawbridge and Ralph Hotere. Drawbridge's *Approach to St André* (1960) reflects both a keen observation of nature—the plane trees that line the roads of rural France—and also a growing knowledge of the etching techniques of French artists such as Pierre Bonnard and André Segonzac. Around the time he made this engraving, Drawbridge was studying printmaking in Paris with S. W. Hayter and Johnny Friedlander. Technical knowledge and experience gained during this period provided the basis for Drawbridge's subsequent printmaking. By way of his subsequent career as a teacher, this knowledge was disseminated widely through New Zealand in the 1970s and 80s—an important and vigorous period in this country's printmaking.

In the early 1960s Ralph Hotere worked at Vence, and returned to the south of France in 1978. Both sojourns were among the most productive times in his life. Hotere has always maintained that the Midi is a part of the world he feels completely at home in. Heraldic symbols from Mediterranean cultures have recurred in his work since the latter trip—see *Les*

John Drawbridge, *Approach to St André*, 1960, etching and mezzotint,
600 x 497 mm, collection of the artist (photograph by Michael Roth)

Saintes Maries de la Mer (1986), with its heart/cross motif. The black rainbow alludes to the shadow cast by the *Rainbow Warrior* bombing the previous year. Elsewhere Hotere incorporated into his work quotations from the Provençal novelist Jean Giono, whom he was reading avidly at the time.

The world renewed

The introductory note to Bishop Pompallier's 1888 *Early History of the Catholic Church in Oceania* sums up the attitude of the Catholic mission in New Zealand: 'Here all is new—all is fresh and modern . . .'.[15] Paradoxically, the notion of the 'modern' which drew French missionaries and colonists out here is a large part of the reason New Zealand writers and artists have ventured off in the direction of France. While the South Pacific might be the New World, any notion of the 'new' or 'modern' in art has, until relatively recently anyway, had to be sourced in the Old World. If Matisse and Gauguin had dreams of the Pacific as a source of renewal, a way forward, it is equally true that, for generations of New Zealand artists, France—with its museums and galleries—has presented a comparable education in the extraordinary, a new set of creative possibilities.

While New Zealand is unlikely ever to be as present in the collective French mind as France is in New Zealand's, the increasing profile of New Zealand films, literature and music in Paris bodes well for the future. Janet Frame is acknowledged by the French as a major international writer and a diverse assortment of New Zealand novels are currently translated into French, among them Witi Ihimaera's *Whale Rider*, Alan Duff's *Once Were Warriors*, Geoff Cush's *Son of France* and the books of Chad Taylor. The novels of Witi Ihimaera, Patricia Grace and Keri Hulme are taught in French universities. Katherine Mansfield's stories and journals are constantly being reissued, retranslated, commentated upon and generally talked up in Paris. A number of New Zealanders have made their lives in that city, among them the painter Douglas McDiarmid, singer-songwriter Graeme Allwright, poet Andrew Johnston

Ralph Hotere, *Les Saintes Maries de la Mer*, 1986, lithograph,
540 x 375 mm, courtesy of Paper Graphica, Christchurch

and, most recently, saxophonist Lucien Johnson (son of the 1988 Katherine Mansfield Memorial Fellow, Louis Johnson, who appears below). A mural by Wellingtonian/sometime-Parisian Sarah Wilkins (who produced the cover art for this book) graces the wall of an apartment building in the 11th arrondissement.

While, as Allen Curnow has it in 'A Nice Place on the Riviera', 'the annual New / Zealander sweats / brief tenure out', at the other end of the globe the Randell Cottage Creative New Zealand Writers Residency now enables a French writer to provide a counterpoint to that. With Charles Juliet's *Au pays du long nuage blanc: Journal, Wellington août 2003–janvier 2004* published early in 2005 by the prestigious imprint POL, and with New Zealand featuring in the recent fictions and non-fictions of Nadine Ribault and Pierre Furlan, the future traffic in ideas and inspiration should be far more two-sided. Acknowledging the accomplishments of the past, we now find ourselves at the beginning of an immensely promising phase in the literary and artistic relationship between France and New Zealand.

Jenny Bornholdt and Gregory O'Brien
Wellington, April 2005

Notes

1 *Letters of Frances Hodgkins*, ed. Linda Gill, Auckland: Auckland University Press,1993, pp. 377–8.
2 New Zealand has also occupied a place in the French imagination, be it as South Seas idyll, far-flung Catholic mission, an island-machine for creating rugby players or—as the anonymous author of the pornographic novel *Cruelle Zélande* (Paris: Jean-Jacques Pauvert, 1978) imagines—the home of a tribe of erotomaniacs hell-bent on kidnapping visitors and initiating them into savage and sordid pursuits.
3 C. K. Stead, *Paris*, Auckland: Auckland University Press/Oxford University Press, 1984, p.6.
4 M. K. Joseph, *Imaginary Islands*, Auckland: Whitcombe & Tombs, 1950, p. 45.
5 Peter Bland, 'Gauguin in Auckland 1891', in *Let's Meet: poems 1985–2003*, Wellington: Steele Robert, 2003. The exact date of Gauguin's stay has been

The Colour of Distance

108 rue J.P. TIMBAUD 75011

Sarah Wilkins, mural in rue Jean-Pierre Timbaud, Paris, commissioned by
La Mairie de Paris in 1998 (photograph by Luc Quelin)

confirmed as 19–29 August 1895. His signature appears in the Auckland City Art Gallery's visitors' book and his name features on the passenger list of the SS *Tarawera*, on which he arrived in Auckland.

6 Bronwen Nicholson (with contributions by Roger Neich, Roger Blackley, Jonathan Mane-Wheoki and Richard Wolfe), *Gauguin and Maori Art*, Auckland: Godwit/Auckland Art Gallery, 1995.

7 *Ibid.*, p. 77.

8 Contributors to the exhibition were: Nigel Brown, Bronwynne Cornish, Judy Darragh, Murray Grimsdale, Pat Hanly, Paul Hartigan, Paul Jackson, Barry Lett, Lauren Lysaght, Jan Nigro, Gregory O'Brien, Claudia Pond-Eyley, John Pule, Paul Radford, John Robinson, Jeff Thomson, Pauline Thompson, Warren Viscoe, Pamela Wolfe. A parallel project involving New Zealand writers, *Beneath the Surface* (ed. Harriet Allen), was published by Random House NZ later in the year and reproduced some works from this exhibition.

9 Jonathan Bywater, 'Derrida was here', *Landfall 202*, November 2001, Dunedin: Otago University Press, p. 181.

10 *Le Toucher, Jean-Luc Nancy*, Paris: Galilée, 2000.

11 Letter from Robin Maconie to Gregory O'Brien, 24 February 2005.

12 Sarah Shieff, *Talking Music; conversations with New Zealand musicians*, Auckland: Auckland University Press, 2002, p. 65.

13 The exhibition 'Len Lye' was shown at the Centre Pompidou, 5–30 April, before touring to the Musée D'Art Moderne et Contemporain, Strasbourg, and Fresnoy, Studio National Des Arts Contemporains. The exhibition was accompanied by a major catalogue publication in French and English.

14 Roger Horrocks, *Len Lye: a biography*, Auckland: Auckland University Press, 2001, p. 387.

15 Jean Baptiste François Pompallier, *Early History of the Catholic Church in Oceania* (translated by Arthur Herman), with an introduction by John Edmund Luck, Auckland: H. Brett, 1888, p. 6.

Acknowledgements

Thanks to Jean-Michel Marlaud, Ambassador of France, and others at the Embassy, especially Typhaine Biard-Hamon, François Lucas, Elsa Thual and Margery Vacle; Jean Anderson for her excellent translations; Roger Horrocks, Pierre Furlan, Andrew Johnston, Bill Manhire, Dylan Horrocks, Fergus Barrowman, Elizabeth Caffin, Sarah Wilkins, Robin Maconie, Michael Jackson, Andrea Hotere, staff of City Gallery Wellington, Marion Maguire, Karl Stead and Paul Millar. We are grateful to all the writers and artists who have contributed to this project.

Part One

Continental Drift

New Zealanders in France

M. K. Joseph

M. K. Joseph (1914–81) is best known for his novel *A Soldier's Tale* (1976), an account of love and violence set in France during the final months of the Second World War. The novel was filmed in 1988 by Larry Parr. As well as another five novels and considerable literary criticism, Joseph published poetry. His selected poems, *Inscription on a Paper Dart*, appeared in 1974. His first two collections, *Imaginary Islands* (1950) and *The Living Countries* (1959), include poems which refer back to his time soldiering in Europe. In a 1979 memoir, Joseph chose to recall his war experiences as 'fairly mild': 'In memory, we were always stationed in unspoilt villages; duties were light; the local people were friendly in a reserved sort of way; there seemed to be always a neighbouring lake or freshwater swimming-pool to spend long sunny afternoons in, and service clubs stocked with lager and white wine for the long golden evenings.' *A Soldier's Tale* and the sonnet 'Drunken Gunners', however, bespeak a darker, more traumatic experience.

Drunken Gunners (Normandy 1944)

The gunners move like figures in a dance
Harmoniously at their machine that kills
Quite casually beyond the shadowed hills
Under the blue and echoing air of France.
The passing driver watches them askance:
'Look at the beggars—pickled to the gills.'
Yet bodies steadied in parade-ground skills
Correct the tottering mind's intemperance.

Housed under summer leafage at his ease,
Artillery board set up, the captain sees
His rule connect two dots a league apart
And throws destruction at hypotheses,
Wishing that love had ministers like these
To strike its distant enemy to the heart.

Wissant-sur-Mer

The slanted light lay across the channel
Pressing against the cliffs; the children
With bare long legs trod demurely
As cranes, against the gold sky and the great
Lost sandscape of that little beach.
The sand was firm as flesh, rippled and ribbed
Like the layered muscles of a skinned fish.
The gold lodged in each ripple, the grey
And gold lay in the long pools
Among the ridges between tide and tide.

And from those fallen skies we dredged our shrimps.

Fragment of an Autobiography
(Rouen, circa 1922)

For G.F.J.

Ah! que le monde est grande à la clarté des lampes!
Aux yeux du souvenir que le monde est petit!
—Baudelaire, *Le Voyage*

I walked a bare-kneed boy in a black overall
Satchel in hand through the lavender streets
The Monet-coloured streets of the evening city
And out of all a year in my life I remember

Edible things, hot rolls and chocolate
Arcachon oysters eaten by candle-light
At street-stalls; cakes of cream and essences
In the pastrycook's of the Rue de l'Horloge
(Under the clock), delicatessen food
For Sunday mornings, and after Cathedral mass
In the café with my father playing dominoes.

The gravelled playground (vast
In time's distorting lens)
Where we grazed our knees. *La Canne*
The discipline-master. Reward-cards
And a blotted copying-book.
Reading with steel-engravings, sugar almonds
The teacher gave out on her godson's nameday.

There were barges on the river and one noon
When the sun touched to gold and rainbows
Oil and the flotsam on the broken water—
'Look, a diver going down. *En francais*
Il s'appelle un scaphandrier.'
Barges and pools of oil, the copper dome
Descending into a river full of gluculent bubbles.

M.K. Joseph   31

Winter afternoon. An old red-nosed man
Sells hot chestnuts in paper bags
From a stove shaped like a steam-engine.
The Thursday cinema—*Nanook*, the Musketeers,
Max Linder, Fairbanks, *Quo Vadis?*
Where indeed. Shadows we are.

History was Jeanne's cell, narrow arches,
Armed men on all sides, and that market place.
Never alone until the death on the faggots
And a soldier's cross made of two sticks
(But the heart, they say, would not burn).
There is more history now: the city
Of Jeanne, Monet, Flaubert,
The Norman city
Is martyred and lives, strong in ruins
And always the river has barges and divers
The playground is gravelled
Children running and falling and laughing
A solemn boy in the café plays dominoes
The hour of the burning the hour of the bomber
And the hour of a boy in my mind.

The weather-vanes point to the four
Winds and the four city weathers
Trees are green trees are brown trees are bare
But always that boy in my brain
Walks through the lavender streets
The trees scribbled like Chinese ink
On a mist of evening the squares being empty
And the streets long and the lamps aglow
Long ago.

The Colour of Distance

Charles Brasch

Best known as the founder-editor of *Landfall*, Charles Brasch (1909–73) was also a poet and arts patron. Between studying at Oxford (1927–31) and returning to New Zealand permanently after the Second World War, Brasch was largely based in London, from where he travelled to Egypt on three occasions and to cities throughout Europe. This extract is from his memoir of his early life, *Indirections*.

from Indirections

I stayed for July and early August with a family in Tours. My hostess, voluminous and voluble, started talking as soon as I arrived and talked to me solidly for two days without requiring a syllable in reply; then she began asking questions, and found that I had not understood a single word. I had been fairly well grounded at Waitaki, but had not heard French spoken. Now listening and talking most of the day and night, and reading French, and hearing no English, I soon learned to follow, and even to speak, fairly fast in the end although very badly. I saw the chateau country and its famous monuments, admired and enjoyed them, but was not moved as by Italy; partly because the styles of architecture were unfamiliar and did not touch me in any direct way— Chinon was poetical, Chenonceaux seemed merely elegant in a way that was little to my taste.

I was flattered one day to be asked by some Americans whether I was Italian. At night we sat in a café with our single drinks that lasted for the evening while Madame told me about the *habitués* and her neighbours and made me talk in turn. She took me to her daughter's wedding at Alençon, where I was made useful by being put in charge of a rich female relation whom none of the family liked but who had to be placated. She was squat and plain and not young—I being chosen specially for her, she was told, as a young and interesting foreigner; I had to escort her into the church, and sit beside her at the feast afterwards, where I first met lobster and was baffled how to eat it. If only I had stayed in Tours twice as long, I might have solidified my grasp of French.

I went back to France a year later, and with my cousin Erik took a summer course at the Sorbonne. But I chose badly, taking a course in French history which did very little to improve my French, while Erik more wisely took one in the language. Paris in July and August is too hot for comfort; we gasped in the exhausting blinding streets by day, and wilted by night sitting naked in our airless pension room trying to prepare work for the next day. We saw all we could of Paris. I grew to love Notre Dame, and the towering, rustling poplars by the Seine, and the Musée Cluny, and admired Rodin while only half understanding him. I can recall almost no painting in Paris from that visit, although we certainly went to the Louvre a number of times. It may have been then that I so admired one body of work which was completely new to me, the wonderful Khmer figures of the Musée Guimet, and felt first the inwardness of compassion that moulds the greatest works of Buddhist art.

Paris did not win me; it seemed too self-absorbed, engrossed in its own mystique, its wholly French *gloire*, implicitly excluding and denying everything except itself. Yet Notre Dame was part of Paris; and Chartres and Beauvais, neither far away, were allies and more than allies of Notre Dame. Colin had prepared me for Chartres, which I was to see again with him. We thought it the crowning point of Gothic; we read Henry Adams on it; we had pictures of its statues and its windows, by which for a time I measured all other works of the kind. It has greater austerity than most Italian and most English churches, due in part to its exposed wind-swept position at the top of the hilly town, amidst wide plains; that helps to give it a sense of being a sacred place, a sanctuary, which few churches possess, not Amiens, nor Bourges, nor Notre Dame, nor, I guess, Rheims. And not Beauvais. Beauvais is breath-taking, inside and out. It does in architecture what some of the figures at Chartres do in sculpture, especially the King of Judah and his companions; but it goes further still, to the perilous limits of possibility, as its history shows. I was to find men who seemed to have gone the same extreme way when

I met the last of the Samaritans at their synagogue in Nablus
a few years later: very tall emaciated fine-drawn men with
skin of transparent ivory, slow of movement, over-refined,
exhausted with inbreeding, the end of a race.

Charles Brasch

Frederick Page

Frederick Page (1905–83) was a university professor of music, critic and pianist. Born in Lyttelton, Page studied composition at the Royal College of Music in London, 1935–38. In 1945 he was appointed lecturer in music at Victoria University College, Wellington, where he was instrumental in the establishment of a forward-thinking music school which, as J. M. Thomson writes, 'became a beacon to the young, a powerful force within the musical community and something of an irritant to more traditional institutions'.

from **A Musician's Journal** (1958)

In Paris, Unesco was running a conference of East-West music. This was something of a flat dive; the French spent time talking about what the conference should talk about; those from beyond Istanbul, no doubt on travel grants, simply came to play their piece and disappear; when they did stay to read a paper it was bewilderingly unclear. Japanese music was now dull, now enchanting, always with a sense of courtesy, of dedication, a sense that music is not something to be snatched at, but approached as a rite, that one should prepare the way for the god. A Vietnamese simply sat down and made music from seemingly what was to hand; he would have made music from an old tin can and a toothpick. Easiest of all on the ear was the music from India; as always, beguiling, relaxing, intoxicating, refreshing. A delegate from Chile asked most pertinently what was meant by these terms East and West. 'Why all this European fuss: music is music, why not let's listen to it?' This did not go down at all well: the Europeans looked well-manneredly puzzled; I, almost alone applauded him. One evening, following Indian music, came two works by Boulez, *Le Marteau sans maître* and one of the *Mallarmé Improvisations*. I found myself moved to tears by the freshness and purity of this music. One could only say that Mallarmé, and Debussy, live. A fashionable audience again made rapidly for the exit, a well-known conductor blowing his top at the absurdity of the

The Colour of Distance

music we had been listening to. The players had vanished and there was Boulez on the stage, a lone figure, putting together the parts of his scores. Nothing for it but to bowl up to him and ask if I might call on him. He was surprised to hear that we had the scores of his *Structures* on our shelves at Victoria. He then lived on that island in the middle of the Seine where I imagine the rich and the less rich live in amity.

I climbed five flights of dreadful wooden stairs to his room. His English was not good, my French was wretched but with a spot of German we managed. I had been the previous night to *Don Giovanni* at the Paris Opera which was unbelievably bad. Musicians in the pit played as though they personally detested Mozart. Cross-legged with boredom, they were still taking it out on him for his unhappiness in Paris in 1778. There was a passably good dry French tenor, an old black pansy for the Don, three ladies, screechingly unseductive, ladies and gentlemen of the ballet who seemed to be making something up as they went along, the chorus was ludicrous, the décor silly. I retailed this horrid story. 'Now you know' was Boulez's comment, 'what it is like for a musician to live in Paris'. As a young man, he told me, he and others found the whole atmosphere of opera and orchestral music in Paris insupportable. Determined to have their own music played, to hear the music of Monteverdi and Webern, they formed their own society and appealed for subscribers. They started off with two hundred which made our efforts in Wellington, by comparison in 1946 quite praiseworthy. 'Monsieur Boulez, I would like to play your music back in New Zealand' I said to him. 'I am a fairly competent pianist but when I opened your *Structures* the difficulties of reading it were so formidable that I nearly fainted'. 'Monsieur' he replied with a blend of seriousness and amusement, 'vous commençez'. The answer delighted me, but I countered further. 'You write for guitar, marimba, bass flute, E flat clarinet, for odd instruments. We haven't got such players or instruments in the country, what then?' 'Monsieur, we too had these difficulties in Paris, we too had no players but we found them, trained them and now have a group keen to play this music'. Faced with this integrity my questions seemed flabby and feeble.

He arranged for me to pick up copies of his scores, invited me to a private performance of his first Piano Sonata, which I had been playing around with at home. The private performance turned out to be the Sonata, bracketed with Schoenberg's op. 4 songs and the *Book of the Hanging Gardens* sung with diamond clarity by a French soprano. The Sonata, played by the composer, I found baffling and incomprehensible. I could only acknowledge its force, its intensity and vigour. To the French these qualities are virtues. The audience of some hundred and twenty was two-thirds men. The house, on the Avenue Foch, had the quietness that now comes from wealth. Set out was a lovely Courbet with a swathe of heavy blue velvet hung about its frame and a T'ang horse, on the walls were abstracts by Poliakoff and de Stael. Chairs were whisked away, tables appeared, we sat down to eat delectable food, drink incomparable wine. I was touched by the beautiful manners of the French at my table towards a stranger who spoke such execrable French as I. They were generous and courteous in bringing me into their circle.

Cilla McQueen

Born in Birmingham, England, in 1949, Cilla McQueen has lived mainly in Dunedin and is now based further south in Bluff. McQueen has an MA in French literature from Otago University, where her studies included the works of Samuel Beckett, Eugene Ionesco and the Theatre of the Absurd. She was a French teacher in Dunedin girls' schools from 1971 to 1984, when she began writing full-time after receiving the Robert Burns Fellowship in 1985. McQueen was married to painter Ralph Hotere from 1974-87. They travelled to France in 1978 with their daughter Andrea.

Avignon Summer 1978

21.6.78

In our little villa there are three main rooms. And a garden. Outside the kitchen door there is a long terrace shaded by a vine and roses, which make a green leafy roof. There is a long table covered with a cream and red oilcloth, four folding chairs, a hose, rubbish in the corner, boxes and plastic bags, a little carved stone flower trough representing the Nativity. On the outside edge of the terrace grows an old fig tree whose branches stretch out to reach those of an apricot tree at the front of the garden, which has at present a likely harvest of a dozen small apricots. Something has been eating its leaves. Andrea's tent is pitched beneath it; sagging blue and orange, a bright red and white sun umbrella in front of it—Slavia, La Grande Bière d'Alsace. The part of the lawn between the terrace and the apricot tree is dry grass and woodshavings, the odd molehill. Beyond Andrea's tent, on the far side of the apricot tree, is Ralph's domain. He has an old door supported on a plank against the tree where his canvas is spread out on a piece of hardboard, pots of paint, brushes and a cardboard box, bits of wood. A long flex with a naked bulb leads from the house and hangs in the branches. At night the effect is theatrical: Ralph painting under the illuminated apricot. A gravel drive bisects the section. As you enter through the spiked iron gates between their tall concrete posts the house is to your left at the back; the fig tree, the apricot tree, Ralph's working place and Andrea's tent all in front of the house. To the right of the driveway at the back between two big trees a washing-line is strung. The ground is covered with ivy in that corner. In front of the washing-line, a line of old irises, then dry grass, a small pear tree, clumps of thyme, rosemary and fennel. Bordering the garden on the right hand side and along the back standing high behind the house are big trees, birch and acacia and cypress. They are always moving and whispering above us.

27.6.78

The Mistral blew for three days last week. We woke up one morning to a fierce rushing sound, like a continuous surf sweeping down over the roof. The Mistral at its height blows continuously, strong and cold, with no change in direction or intensity. The little house feels solid and warm. It is reasonably sheltered as the wind comes from the north, behind us, but as it sweeps down over the roof it nearly pulls to pieces the vine canopy over the terrace. It is almost impossible to hear yourself speak outside as the big trees, bamboo and grasses make a wild rushing and whistling sound constantly. Looking southwards from the kitchen door we watch a line of tall poplars swaying and sweeping, wild and incredibly supple. They don't break, just give in the wind till they are almost bent double. In front of the poplars and reaching to over half their height are some clumpy leafy trees which are all silver glitter, grey and white, as the undersides of their leaves flicker in the wind, rustling and roaring. And in front of them the tall bamboo shrieks and whistles, wildly tugging itself free of the ground and the moving grasses. Everything is moving to the limit of its capacity, everything is making the loudest possible noise. The trees are clashing furiously, and every other piece of vegetation is making its own particular sound, blending with the snarl of the wind itself as it roars down the Rhône Valley, meeting after miles of water and sparse vegetation our small tree-enshrouded encampment.

After three days of such constant wild effort, the silence is deafening, the sun warm, the air a caress. It stopped in the night, as suddenly as it began, and I woke up to listen for it.

4.7.78

We woke up early this morning. There was a seething and wetly plopping sound of big fat raindrops on to vine and fig leaves—it was raining, gently, heavily, firmly. The oilcloth on the table was shining wet, and the clothes we had left outside were soaking. The vase of sunset-orange roses was overflowing with rain, the roses wide open, brilliant, drinking in all the water. A gentle green watery light filtered through the vines overhead and through the fig leaves; the drops as they fell through the green canopy were like big uncut pale diamonds, or moonstones, reflecting the white sky. All day the sploshing and falling sounds of rain on all surfaces—the hard slap of a big drop on the oilcloth, a hiss on to concrete, a plop on to leaves, a soft swallowing sound on the dry earth.

5.7.78

This morning after the rain it is fresh and sunny. The poplars and the trees in front of them are all clean and winking in the sunlight, the poplars gently swaying out of rhythm. The bamboo is glistening and green, waving majestically like great leafy fans. The light is dappling down through the leaves of the trees and freckling everything with gold moving patches; the shadow of the apricot tree writes hieroglyphics of leaves against the whitewashed wall. The fig tree's branches loop like thick knotty rope, and the dark shapes of the leaves make sharp-edged silhouettes against the pale, bright sky. All the greens! The dark shadowy green underneath the vine above the terrace, the luminous golden green of the leaves pierced by the sun. The fig leaves are black-green against the sky, the bamboo is silver-and-gold green, the wattles are feathery, the birches glittery, and all the leaves are always gently moving so the colours and shapes change subtly all the time. A brilliant point of sunlight strikes through the vine canopy; the sun has risen above the birch trees. It will be hot today.

7.7.78

Today it is windy and bright. Sitting outside at lunchtime it was like being in a storm of glitter. The sunlight filtering down through the vine above us made points of yellow light which jumped and danced wildly as the wind shook the leaves about.

8.7.78

Maurice from the farm down the road brought us some vegetables today. He has a beautiful brown leathery deeply-lined face, and a bright crinkly smile. He shows me how the stalks of the courgettes are still wet, snaps a bean to show how fresh his vegetables are. He will have no more than one glass of rosé with us, before he shakes hands and goes back to work.

9.7.78

The Mistral blew steadily again today, and we made a kite. In the evening when the wind was starting to drop we took it out beside the river and flew it, but the more it flew the more the wind dropped, and it ended up flopping along the gravel. The sun was like an orange searchlight as it went down behind the violet battlements of the ancient fort across the river, the sky all patches of bruised colour as it set. With it went the wind completely, and the birches suddenly turned bright gold, then black and lacy, and rested from the windy day.

10.7.78

It has been a hot and cloudless day, a breeze only slightly rustling the leaves of the trees above us. Early in the evening we sat in the sun in the garden, and the sun above the fig tree shone through the leaves making them glow brilliant green, and casting big floppy shadows on the ground. Now it is still quiet dark night. The cicadas sing incessantly, the trees are holding still their leaves, the air is warm and dry. We are sitting at the long table on the terrace drinking rosé. The white stucco of the house wall looks like the surface of the moon under the outside light. A young vine dislodged by yesterday's wind trails down from the canopy and gently sways. There is a crystal clear violin sonata on the radio.

On ne peut jamais boire un seul pastis ici—on dit 'Tu vas partir en boitant, faut en prendre deux, pour l'equilibre . . .'.

If you only have one pastis you go away with a limp. . . .

11.7.78
Andrea was nine today. We gave her a kite for the Mistral, a recorder for fairy music on quiet nights, multi-coloured bubbles to dance with, some tin soldiers and some paper dolls. We took a picnic lunch and went to the little stony beach on the Gardon, where you can look at the Pont du Gard against a backdrop of dark blue-green bush and sky. There are tourists walking along the top like inquisitive ants. It is overcast but warm. Andrea swims her new somewhat stationary breaststroke in the clear dark green water; shoals of little fish flit over the stones. A party of French schoolchildren splash past in brightly coloured canoes, a hearty German family swim about enthusiastically. Four French cars are parked in a line and there is a complicated lunch served; they sit in their canvas chairs at little camping tables and talk and eat vigorously. A fat pink man stands very still holding a huge surfcasting rod over the still water. Ralph is drawing the Pont du Gard, a brilliant blue dragonfly above his head.

15.7.78
Avignon is apricot in the evening. The battlements of the walls and gates are sharply cut out against the sky; warm, battered old stones. The Rhône flows deep and imperturbable past the old Pont St Bénézet. The bell in the tower on the bridge sings out mellow over the old stones and the water.

20.7.78
There is a wind this evening. A huge full moon rose yellow behind the dark sweeping poplars, and now hangs above them, white and shining, enigmatic and unruffled above the swirling masses of the trees below.

25.7.78

Maurice from the farm calls in sometimes about nine or ten in the evening, and we have a glass of wine. The other night he'd been having a few whiskies in town, and he waxed most patriotic. He does very hard physical work from five in the morning till eight or nine at night, and is paid very little. But it is on and for the land that he works, and he loves and belongs to it entirely. Ah, he says, here in France we are free. I would be the first to stand up and be shot for the name of Liberty. Here we have such Liberty, too much even! Life is simple, France is beautiful, the most beautiful country in the world. You should see my peaches! When they are ready I will bring you some. You'll see. As big as plates! His brown face hatched with wrinkles, checked shirt, bow legs and felt hat ride past during the day as he does errands and delivers vegetables in the basket on the front of his vélo. For outings, he wears a large sports jacket, tie, and slicked-down hair. The first time he appeared in his best clothes, I hardly recognised him. He came to get us on the evening of the 14th July, and took us to watch a magnificent fireworks display over the old Pont St Bénézet and the river. Then he insisted on having several large whiskies in a bar in town. This is my second home, he explained simply as he waved away our money. Everybody knows me here. You'll see. Everybody knows Maurice.

I went to the farm this morning to buy some vegetables for lunch. Maurice took my bag and came back proudly with about twelve kilos of tomatoes and courgettes. I tried to pay him, but he waved the money away. Pay me next time perhaps, he said. Besides, there are some visitors from Belgium. Ah, they say, does the sun shine like this all the time? I say it does, the Midi is the part of the world where the sun shines the most, the sun always shines. For us, when the sky is overcast, there is gloom all around. It is that one up there, that sun of ours, that makes us live. La fiesta, as they say in Spain! These beautiful vegetables, I'll give them to you, take them as a gift. You'll feast like kings. Bon appétit!

27.7.78

We had a picnic on the high rocky white hills near Les Baux, and came home via Arles.

A Turkish-looking blue enamelled dragonfly hovers on a heatwave, shoots backwards, lands momentarily on a sprig of rosemary and disappears, vertical, instantaneous. Behind it the white rocks quiver. The sun rasps down. The cicadas grind it up and leave it to the rocks to throw back again.

Tall black cypresses severely marshal their green and yellow cornfields. The Mistral has made everything lean slightly. Along the road the plane trees stretch their branches out to their partners on the other side, who lean backwards, embarrassed. The trees with little leaves shake and flitter them, throwing the light around.

The sound of the cicadas is the sound the sun makes, ceaselessly grinding out its heat. The dragonflies and butterflies dance, drunkenly, to the rhythm of it.

30.7.78

I walked across the Place du Palais in the mid-afternoon hot sun, the Sunday bells pealing out from Notre Dame des Doms, echoing back and forth between the old stone walls.

2.8.78

Last night I dreamed that we were all three huddled in our bed, listening to screams of children carried on a blast of air down an ancient stone chimney. Someone was roaring and snarling outside and banging on the roof, trying to get in, and the grey ghost of a friend was waiting in the kitchen.

I woke up and went outside. There was thunder, right overhead, and sizzling rain. The trees were thrashing about madly in the wind which swept down from all angles. It was hot. The sky was strangely light. Three o'clock in the morning.

23.8.78

It feels like late summer now. In the morning when I get up there is a mist, and everything is damp from the night's dew. The sky is white, the trees still and silver-grey. Gradually the sun clears the mist away from the sky until it is huge and blue. All day it is hot, and the cicadas sing. As we drove home from the Fontaine de Vaucluse yesterday evening the light was slanting and golden. The trees and vines in the foreground were crystal clear, fading in the middle distance to a misty blue, and the horizon quite vanished in the haze of dark blues and greens, broken by the dark steeples of the cypresses between the vineyards.

29.8.78

This morning I got up at seven o'clock. When I opened the shutters, everything was quiet and white. I could hardly make out the tall shapes of the poplars through the mist, but as I watched it cleared away, revealing the bamboo grey and silver, its fans of leaves motionless and drooping. The poplars were waiting for the sun, and when it began to filter through the disappearing mist they started to move their leaves and sway, very gently, gaining depth and colour as they came into focus. With the day came a little breeze, and the silent sleep of the early morning gave way to the wakeful bustle of the leaves and branches.

1.9.78

Perhaps it is early autumn already. Perhaps still late summer. The dividing line is somewhere between the ripe purple figs swelling and splitting on the ends of the fig tree branches, and the leaves above us which are turning to orange, pink and scarlet patches against the still predominant green. The canopy is less thick now, and the sky shows through. When the wind blows, big bright blots of sunlight scatter all over us as we sit at the table. The paintings hanging on the outside walls change all the time as the shimmering flickering patches dance over them, or rest in starry patterns of light and shade. In the sun their colours are deep and brilliant, dark and secret in the shadow. Now and again a curly brown leaf drops on to the table, or rustles along the concrete with a dry whisper.

5.9.78
At this end of the arc of summer the mornings are cool. The sun sparkles pale and brilliant through the trees on to last night's raindrops hanging on the washing-line. The dying leaves hang quietly. We have eaten nearly all the figs.

Mistral Song, for Ralph

The Mistral blows
The Mistral blows
The first day of the Mistral
My true love said to me
Jesus Christ this wind is strong
See those poplars sweeping?
The second day of the Mistral
My true love said to me
Jesus Christ this wind is strong
See those poplars sweeping
Hear the bamboo whistling
Let's go and look at ancient monuments
But the Mistral followed
The third day of the Mistral
We clenched our eyes and shut our teeth
The branches knocked against the roof
The bamboo whistled
The poplars shrieked
The cypresses rent their branches
We tore our hair out
We let our legs and arms go
And threw our clothes out the windows
We opened the roof and let
The branches take over
The Mistral blows
The Mistral blows
And when we had quite surrendered
It left, nonchalantly,
Whistling vaguely among the grasses.

The Colour of Distance

James K. Baxter

James K. Baxter (1926–72) was a poet, critic and social commentator. 'At Serrières' was written in 1962 and takes its title from the French town Baxter visited in 1937 while travelling in Europe with his family. Baxter refers to his sojourn in France in his 'Letter to Noel Ginn' (1944):

> France: where the Rhône ran under concrete;
> Sewer at bridge-base. Out of the violent sun
> I wrote poems, scrapped poems half-begun
> On clouds and comets. A tower seen from the street:
> Skeletons found there. Bats. Snake at my feet . . .

The town of Serrières made a considerable impact on the ten-year-old poet, and two years later he wrote what scholar Paul Millar believes to be the only poem from that time which refers directly to the European trip—'Serrieres (sans accent)'—a youthful evocation of the town. At various stages of his life Baxter read French poetry avidly, and he was drawn to the idea of the poet as the prophet and alchemist as embodied by Rimbaud and Mallarmé. (Baxter's poem 'The First Communions', published in 1969, is a version 'after Rimbaud'.)

At Serrières

Blue water of the Rhône in its rock bed
Stalling, circling in pools behind
The island lousy with snakes: down I sank
With stones inside my bathing dress
To the mud bottom, to walk like a crab,

All that green summer drank
Air, knowledge. Bitter tough-skinned grapes
In a wild hilltop vineyard,
And the days, the days, like long loaves
Broken in half, as I fished with a cord

And a pierced stone for Yvette, the manager's daughter,
Killing hens in the hotel courtyard.
That castle where my brother broke his arm,
Yes: convolvulus vines, starved ghosts in dungeons . . .
But the family album does not include

The new guitar of sex I kept on twanging
Inside the iron virgin
Of the little smelly dyke, or that Easter Sunday,
Through a chink in the bedclothes, watching my mother
        dressing:
The heavy thighs, the black bush of hair.

Those wild red grapes were bitter
Though you could not tell them, by just looking, from the
        table kind.

Ian Wedde

Meridian Energy Katherine Mansfield Memorial Fellow in 2005, Ian Wedde was born in Blenheim in 1946. He has published twelve collections of poetry, three novels and a vast amount of literary and art criticism. His sequence *Homage to Matisse* (1971) first appeared as a pamphlet from the Amphedesma Press, a shortlived London-based publishing operation comprising Bill Manhire and Kevin Cunningham, and was later incorporated into his first major collection, *Made Over* (1974). Throughout his distinguished career as poet and art writer/curator, Wedde has occupied that typically French interface between the literary and visual arts worlds.

from Homage to Matisse

1. Nature Morte: The Room

Henri Emile Benoît Matisse je vous salue!
Let me tell you a secret.
Your work goes on.
I'd only seen your things in art books
bite sized. I dreamed there was a bright room
in my head somewhere
which you were making real stroke

by counterpointed stroke
& where I would some day retire
to an armchair in the corner:

the final element of a composition
that perfectly described itself.

& three years later saw the first good
real one/   Basle Switzerland:
Still Life With Oysters. As expected

it cleared the room. I sat humming in a corner of/
homesick. Others came & sighed round the walls
searching for deep truffles. Outside

nature was dead.
Civic Swiss had combed her hair for press-releases.
Her rigour was bourgeois & precise.
Children clambered upon her in
mid-summer in knee socks.

Come away Master.
At our place we can still snap life
open like   oysters.
You were one instructor.
Matisse, Matisse.

5. une harmonie d'ensemble

The sun comes up Henri & goes down.
In between is a long split-
legged slow-motion dancer's leap.

Did we break the sound barrier?
I saw cities / chipped stacks of dominoes.
Hah! cried the old crookback
players   slapping down stakes
shaking the last coins in their vest pockets.

Beyond them was the sea moving/
the clonic hips of a loving woman
& a feathered man falling into
her.   She blinked

like a deep blue eye. His image
disappeared in its frank distances.

So be it Henri / so
be it.

Dinah Hawken

Dinah Hawken (born 1943) is a New Zealand poet who lives in Wellington but has had the chance to stay in Geneva for several periods over the last three years. From there, France is a stone's throw away and has been the destination of weekend travel. 'France for the Weekend' is from the journal sequence 'Fighting and Mating in Geneva', which will be included in her forthcoming book *Threatened and Buoyant Like Us*. Her most recent book is *Oh There You Are Tui!: New and Selected Poems* (2001).

France for the Weekend

le 5 Mai

Back in the room. Our first incursion into France was exciting. But for me, cautious in new situations, it is also a relief to be 'home'. How I love to be settled so the inner life can begin.

Le voyage. Drove from Gex up through the Colle de Faucille, which has 3 stars in the Green Guide and is amazingly loopy on the map, into the Jura. To our surprise it was soon snowing and the temperature fast dropping. The Jura despite their flat tops are mountains and the Swiss and French simply cross most mountains by car. The conical trees—the dark green of spruce and fir, and the light green new growth on beech, larch, birch and oak—held light layers of snow. Over the tops we tentatively drove, and then down into the deep fissure or rift on the other side where surprisingly (and bleakly we thought) there was a sizeable town. Morez. The Jura are a series of long parallel ridges and valleys running lengthwise from the Rhône to the Rhine and stepping down in folds to the west, into Burgundy. The small stone villages that had looked so charming in the photographs seemed closed up and isolated in the rain so we headed for the life of a bigger town, Lons le Saunier (19,000). Some charming old streets, especially the Rue de Commerce with its low generous arcades. In a side street we found La Bomboche, packed with locals. The one waiter, wearing tight pants and shiny black shoes, moved with impressive speed and artfully from table to table through the whole evening. Not a hint of tension or irritation. Pour moi, smoked salmon and haricot verts, jambon in cream sauce, lightly cooked legumes and mousse au citron. Un pistiche of local wine. So good. Everyone so alive conversationally that, try as we might, we felt downunder drab.

The next day it was Baume Les Messieurs, the greenest of small stone villages in a reculée, the Cirque de Baume. The long valleys of the Jura often end in a circle of curved-edged, overhanging limestone cliffs: a reculée. I love the word and I love the actuality. The Cirque de Baume has a resurgent spring gushing from the entrance of huge limestone caves and slowing beautifully over a layered cascade. The village itself, with a small monastery for les messieurs, the monks who became happily and decadently wealthy there, is verdant and charming even in the rain. We have booked 'une chambre pour trois personnes' for Rachael's visit.

Samedi le 18 Mai
Aix-les-Bains is a strange decadent place with too many grand hotels from the Belle Epoch standing empty. We are in a 2-star on the edge of the centre of town and have woken up again to rain. We are between seasons. We are not here for La Cure as most other tourists, in their seventies, seem to be. As far as we can work out Les Bains (the Baths) are purely medical for there is no sign of an ordinary public hot pool as in NZ. This afternoon we have been to a small musée—Faure—to see a collection of Impressionist paintings and wonderful small Rodin sculptures. As well we have seen Lamartine's room in Aix-les-Bains where he was living when he fell in love with Julie, Madame Charles, sent by her husband from Paris for La Cure in 1816. She died the following year and in his grief he wrote 'Le Lac':

> O time, suspend your flight,
> and you, propitious hours,
> suspend your course . . . . . .

le 21 Mai

I expect too much from sightseeing and travel. After all, going to Savoie for the weekend for the Génévois is the equivalent of going to the Wairarapa for the weekend from Wellington. And even Switzerland and France have weather. It rained again almost all weekend.

But here in Bellevue! A crow has landed and swayed on the sycamore and a falcon has swooped over. You see I have time. When sightseeing there never seems to be enough time. In a room of Rodin sculptures, not enough time. On a guided tour of the Abbaye de Hautcombe, not enough time. Sightseeing can be like seeing numerous interesting friends at a large party, not *really* talking with anyone, and going home medium-sad. Though the French seem to take their time very nicely. They stroll. They sit and talk and talk like the two elderly men in the central square at Aix-les-Bains or the locals having their two-hour plus Sunday lunch at the Relais du Chantagne in Chindreux. *That*—galantine du canard, mousse de sole, boeuf et champignons etc., fromage de Savoie, sorbet, café—slowed us down.

Generally Aix-les-Bains and particularly the Casino Grande Cercle left us with a feeling of flatness. The beautiful dregs of the C19 jet set. The Panoramic, the Astoria, the Britannique, the Splendide, the Excelsior, the Royal. The attractive dark woman in the Casino, all day at the poker machines, in a trance. At 11.30 pm there was a clattering of coins and she scooped them out into her big plastic container, handful after handful, staring ahead, as if she was scooping up handfuls of desert sand. Then wearily, slowly, with no energy for the sleeves, she pulled her jacket over her shoulders and roused herself to get up. A defeated 30-year-old. Overhead, above the hundred-plus flashing machines, arched the extraordinary and fine mosaic ceilings of the Belle Epoch.

C. K. Stead

Since retiring from Auckland University in 1986, C. K. Stead (born 1932) has travelled frequently to France, where much of his 2004 novel *Mansfield* is set. An earlier novel, *Villa Vittoria*, is set on the Ligurian Riviera, not far from Menton, where Stead was Mansfield Fellow in 1972. Stead's translation of Apollinaire's great poem 'Pont Mirabeau' was published in his 1983 collection, *Poems of a Decade*. His sequence of poems, *Paris*—with drawings by Gregory O'Brien—appeared in 1984, and was followed by a coda, 'Paris: the end of the story', in his 1988 collection, *Between*. Other notable France-related poetry by Stead includes sections of the two sequences, 'Walking Westward' (1979) and 'Yes, T. S.' (1982). 'Deconstructing the Rainbow Warrior' (1988) neatly summarises his response to both the *Rainbow Warrior* bombing and the advent of French theory.

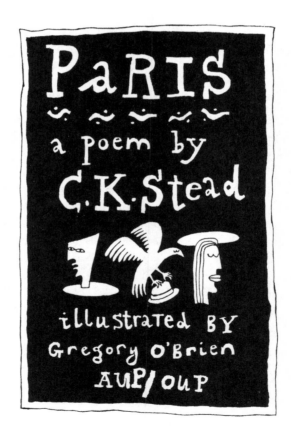

from **Paris**

1

City so long announced come home to my dreams.
These are the days of my defeat when I long for
your anonymity, your bidets. Light me a whiffling candle,
pour me a small black coffee, send down-river your glass barges,
let your new immaculate wheels put forth on their tracks
to St Lazare, tell your best-breasted girls to expect me,
your clowns before the Beaubourg to hold their fire;
ask the crisp ready leaves of St Germain-en-Laye
to delay their plunge, the plumbing everywhere to hold back
its last laugh, the cars to polish their hubcaps.
Already stone angels in the cemetery of Père Lachaise
are trying their wings against the rumour of a wind from the north.
It will be late summer, it will be autumn, it will be almost
winter and it will be winter. It will not be spring.
City so long undreamed, please look to your laurels.
Here there's nothing but the spite of choked passages
and green bananas, nothing but the spirit of Palmerston North
going to bed in lambskins. Paris, summon me to your table.
I invite myself to your board, I accept your invitation
and my defeat. Paris, put yourself in the picture.

7

It is because we're all to die that we visit Paris—
not that we want salvation or think eternity possible
or believe more fervently in God than in the bathroom,
nor in Notre Dame with its burning bushes of candles,
but that this is an arcane language we can turn an ear to
as to the thrush on a wet evening, knowing more or less
its import without understanding. This and the sense that
not being gods or angels we have slipped right by
the frontier guards and are walking invisible in a heaven
of plausible dimension leading by cobbled backstreets
to the breadsticks, berets and bicycles of favourite old movies.
Paul Gauguin came to our ocean for similar reasons
and the blood still shows on the walls of the Beaubourg.
Night is certainly a laboratory in which are made
colours of the trees, the river and the morning sky,
and you'll need your wits about you walking home
through the cold dawn without a visible presence
seeking only the safest route to the Rue Madame.
To the riddle of Life the best short answer may be Death
but not desiring it we can always settle for Paris.

10

Now is the night we used to call Symbol of Death
but there's water through branches and lights and stars on
        the water.
Showing at the cinema on the far side of the square
is your movie with Catherine Deneuve—yes already it's made.
She kisses you in a mirror and the cats on the mansard
quote Rimbaud at the moon, which answers in French.
The glass doors open inward, the shutters push out,
and there beyond the balcony railing it runs
the silver ribbon of your thought rebuffed by the light.
Here you can see why Chagall's lovers float up
through branches to join the stars—it's the shortest route
to a high old time and not as difficult as walking.
In the Rue Mazarine your table is waiting in a window.
Will she be there with her neat and busy bush?
Go out among these hands that are pure conjecture.
As wine touches the tongue, as the eyes exchange,
as a voice caresses an uncomprehending ear,
do not neglect to dictate these informal strictures
with all their whims of glass, their glosses on lust,
to the Paris of Paris that's nobody's dream but your own.

Andrew Johnston

After leaving Wellington in 1996, Andrew Johnston (born 1963) settled in Paris, where he lives with his wife and son. He works as an editor on the *International Herald Tribune* and edits the literary website www.thepage.name. His third and most recent collection of poems is *Birds of Europe* (2000).

At St-Romphaire

What's cooking? The glass lid
lets you in: a fish
simmering, with
peppercorns, fresh herbs.

The table's made from a cider press,
a slab of dark grain with hazelnuts,
artichokes, aubergines, grapes.
In the garden the light's so bright

you shut your eyes, but it comes right through
so you open them again: a black shape,
black as a shiver, over the lettuces—
a shadow, or the butterfly? A fritillary?

The Silver-Washed. The Queen of Spain.
A filament. A living descendant.
Blink and it vanishes. What's
in the pot? Look through the lid.

Georges

Entrée, plat, salade, fromage, then
Georges falls asleep on the couch,

wakes to find the eyes on him of
four generations. *Merde*,

he mutters. He wants some peace.
Dessert is *Iles Flottantes*

in silence. Through the window
a man is furiously

tearing up weeds with a rake. It's all right,
says Isabelle, we know him.

At Angey

Mamie, Mémère
wade through the house—the years

come up to their waists, some days
the years come up to their shoulders

floating photographs from the mantel—
dead and living lit by the same light—

and when the years are thickest,
you imagine Mamie, Mémère—

as woodsmoke spreads like milk in the morning air—
push off and gently swim from room to room

because you know it's not like that—time
wrecks their knees and bends their backs, and

when the years rise high enough to carry them,
the years will carry them away.

Bonjour la France

for Peter Black

As willows weep and lilies pose,
I see the artist's landscape decompose,

I see standers and waiters escape their fate,
I see a whole continent looking away

I see the light betray Jesus
and Cool Water Woman,

and because the lens reflects
your fine grey sense

I see the hand of circumstance
everywhere. Bonjour la France.

Andrew Johnston

Peter Black

Born in Christchurch in 1948, photographer Peter Black traveled in France for the first time in 1998. Works from the resulting folio, 'Bonjour la France', were shown in the exhibition 'Peter Black— Real Fiction' at City Gallery Wellington, March–June 2003, and reproduced in *Sport 30: Peter Black—Real Fiction*. *Sport 15: White Horse, Black Dog* (1995) was devoted to Black's sequence 'Moving Pictures', and literary responses to it. If Black's work has been most evidently influenced by Robert Frank and other American photographers, while working in France Black felt the presence of Cartier-Bresson and Brassai looming, he says, over his shoulder. In hindsight, he discerns a faint echo of the great French photographic tradition in these images.

from **Bonjour la France**

demander à l'intérieur

Mary Macpherson

Mary Macpherson (born in Dunedin, 1952) has produced extensive work in the field of photography as well as poetry. She is one of four poets featured in *Millionaire's Shortbread* (2003) and has published a collection, *The Inland Eye* (1998). Just as Macpherson accompanied Peter Black on his tour of France, this poem accompanied Black's 'Bonjour la France' photographs in a slip-cased limited edition.

Continents
(*Musée d'Océanie*)

Fish circle in tiny lit oceans;
a boy presses his boat to
a sea of fluttering gills.
You love the names of continents
and how they are so far away.
A woman in a green dress
holds her girl's hand and sings.
Then you are in a forest of dried
leaves, scents & old rocks,
a bird calls—sweet sweet, but
you don't know it, can't name it.
You wait under trees
uncertain of your location.

Elizabeth Smither

Born in New Plymouth in 1941, Elizabeth Smither has published many volumes of poetry, along with four books of short stories and three novels, most recently *The Sea Between Us* (2003). Smither's poems range widely around the world of books, ideas and things. 'The French translation' first appeared in her 1989 collection, *A Pattern of Marching*.

The French translation

'Did you get a nurse and an ambulance?'
I was slightly better at it and with insight
Had unravelled a rather boring landscape description
A word I took for bracken, a stream in its midst
But no accident requiring medical intervention.

What to say? 'I may quite well be wrong.'
In the bracken lay the body of our French mistress
And her black bicycle with its basket wrecked.
Across the river murmurous sounds that grew
And nearby, what we agreed on, *un lapin*.

Elizabeth Knox

Holder of the Katherine Mansfield Memorial Fellowship in 1999, Elizabeth Knox (born 1959) is one of New Zealand's leading novelists. Her international breakthrough, *The Vintner's Luck*, is set in Burgundy. It appeared in 1998, and was translated into French by Pierre Furlan and published as *La veine du vigneron* in 2003.

from The Vintner's Luck

1808 Vin bourru *(new wine)*

A week after midsummer, when the festival fires were cold, and decent people were in bed an hour after sunset, not lying dry-mouthed in dark rooms at midday, a young man named Sobran Jodeau stole two of the freshly bottled wines to baptise the first real sorrow of his life. Though the festival was past, everything was singing, frogs making chamber music in the cistern near the house, and dark grasshoppers among the vines. Sobran stepped out of his path to crush one insect, watched its shiny limbs flicker then finally contract, and sat by the corpse as it stilled. The young man glanced at his shadow on the ground. It was substantial. With the moon just off full and the soil sandy, all shadows were sharp and faithful.

Sobran slid the blade of his knife between the bottle neck and cork, and slowly eased it free. He took a swig of the *friand*, tasted fruit and freshness, a flavour that turned briefly and looked back over its shoulder at the summer before last, but didn't pause, even to shade its eyes. The wine turned thus for the first few mouthfuls, then seemed simply 'a beverage', as Father Lesy would say, the spinsterish priest from whom Sobran and his brother, Léon, had their letters. The wine's now pure chemical power poured from Sobran's gut into his blood. He felt miserable, over-ripe, well past any easy relief.

Céleste was the daughter of a poor widow. She worked for Sobran's mother's aunt, fetched between the kitchen and parlour, was quicker than the crippled maid, yet was 'dear':

'Run upstairs, *dear* . . .'. Céleste kept the old lady company, sat with her hands *just so*, idle and attentive, while Aunt Agnès talked and wound yarn. At sixteen Sobran might have been ready to fall in love with her—now, at eighteen, it seemed his body had rushed between them. When he looked at Céleste's mouth, her shawled breasts, the pink fingertips of her hand curled over the top of the embroidery frame as she sat stitching a hunting-scene fire-screen, Sobran's prick would puff up like a loaf left to prove, and curve in his breeches as tense as a bent bow. Like his friend, Baptiste, Sobran began to go unconfessed for months. His brother Léon looked at him with distaste and envy, their mother shrugged, sighed, seemed to give him up. Then Sobran told his father he meant to marry Céleste—and his father refused him permission.

The elder Jodeau was angry with his wife's family. Why, he wanted to know, hadn't his son been told? The girl didn't exactly set snares, but she was fully conscious of her charms. Sobran was informed that Céleste's father had died mad—was quite mad for years, never spoke, but would bark like a dog. Then at midsummer an uncle, in his cups, put a tender arm around Sobran's shoulder and said don't—don't go near her, he could see how it was, but *that* cunt was more a pit than most, a pit with slippery sides. 'Mark my words.'

At the service after midsummer, in a church full of grey faces, queasiness, and little contrition, Céleste had looked at Sobran, and seemed to know he knew—not that he'd either asked or promised anything—but her stare was full of scorn, and seemed to say, 'Some lover *you* are.' Sobran had wanted to weep, and wanted, suddenly, not to overcome Céleste, to mount a marital assault, but to surrender *himself*. And, wanting, he ached all over. When Céleste spoke to him after the service there was ice in her mouth. And when, in his great-aunt's parlour, she handed him a glass of Malaga, she seemed to curse him with her toast—'*Your health*'—as though it was his health that stood between them.

Sobran got up off the ground and began to climb towards the ridge. The vineyard, Clos Jodeau, comprised two slopes of a hill that lay in the crooked arm of a road which led through the village of Aluze and on past Château Vully on the banks of the river Saône. At the river the road met with a greater road, which ran north to Beaune. When the two slopes of Clos Jodeau were harvested, the grapes of the slope that turned a little to the south were pressed at Jodeau, and the wine stored in the family's small cellar. The remainder of the harvested grapes were sold to Château Vully. The wine of Clos Jodeau was distinctive and interesting, and lasted rather better than the château's.

On the ridge that divided the slopes grew a row of five cherry trees. It was for these that Sobran made, for their shelter, and an outlook. Inside his shirt and sitting on his belt, the second bottle bumped against his ribs. He watched his feet; and the moon behind, over the house, pushed his crumbling shadow up the slope before him.

Last Sunday he had left Aunt Agnès's door before his family, only to go around the back to look in the door to the kitchen, where he knew Céleste had taken refuge. The door stood open. She was stooped over a sieve and pail as the cook poured soured milk into a cheese cloth to catch the curds. Céleste gathered the corners of the cloth and lifted it, dripping whey. She wrung it over the bucket. Then she saw Sobran, gave the cloth another twist and came to the door with the fresh cheese dripping on the flags and on to her apron. Her hands, slick with whey and speckled with grainy curds, didn't pause – as she looked and spoke one hand gripped and the other twisted. She told him he must find himself a wife. In her eyes he saw fury that thickened their black, her irises so dark the whites seemed to stand up around them like, in an old pan, enamel around spots worn through to iron. His desire took flight, fled but didn't disperse. Sobran knew then that he wanted forgiveness and compassion—*her* forgiveness and compassion, and that nothing else would do.

Sobran paused to drink, drank the bottle off and dropped it. He was at the cherry trees; the rolling bottle scattered some fallen fruit, some sunken and furred with dusty white mould. The air smelled sweet, of fresh and fermenting cherries and, oddly strong here, far from the well, a scent of cool fresh water. The moonlight was so bright that the landscape had colour still.

Someone had set a statue down on the ridge. Sobran blinked and swayed. For a second he saw what he *knew*—gilt, paint and varnish, the sculpted labial eyes of a church statue. Then he swooned while still walking forward, and the angel stood quickly to catch him.

Sobran fell against a warm, firm pillow of muscle. He lay braced by a wing, pure sinew and bone under a cushion of feathers, complicated and accommodating against his side, hip, leg, the pinions split around his ankle. The angel was breathing steadily, and smelled of snow. Sobran's terror was so great that he was calm, a serenity like that a missionary priest had reported having felt when he found himself briefly in the jaws of a lion. There was an interval of warm silence; then Sobran saw that the moon was higher and felt that his pulse and the angel's were walking apace.

Sobran looked up.

Lloyd Jones

Katherine Mansfield Memorial Fellow in 1989, Lloyd Jones (born 1955) published his verse-novel *The Book of Fame* in 2000. Much acclaimed on home turf, the imagined account of the 1905 All Black tour of France won the Deutz Medal for Fiction at the Montana New Zealand Book Awards. The narrative begins in New Zealand then sails to England, with a brisk interlude on the continent, where the legendary team hammers the French Fifteen.

from **The Book of Fame**

Winter flattened the fields right to the grey walls of farm cottages. Out of that scene Paris arrived: between looking down and up again a whole city appeared.

Paris was caught in a freeze.
We stood outside Gare du Nord, stomping and breaking up the ice and watching the cabbies try to pick up their fallen horses.
Our ears pricked up at the names we heard—'Anand, Suzette, Catérine'.
The horses looked prettier than ours.
We decided we liked Paris.
We liked it for not being Wales or England.
We especially liked the way women in the streets kissed men on both cheeks.
We thought we could get used to that.
There were no brass bands.
No officials.
No policemen on horses.
No gaping crowds.

There were the usual snail and frog jokes & jokelettes; lively discussion on what we were prepared to eat and what we would point blank refuse, and so on. Corbett, usually a retiring debater, made violent gestures of swiping the tablecloth and throwing down his table napkin in disgust outside the Gare du Nord.

But that evening at dinner, we found ourselves making odd announcements; Cunningham, for example, waving a slice of tomato on the end of his fork and declaring, 'Now this *is* a tomato.' But we knew what he meant; Corbett, Glasgow, Newton, nodding, their mouths too full of tuna flakes and oil and chopped spring onions for them to speak.

Mister Dixon treated us to cognac, and afterwards, in the lounge of the St Petersburg Hotel, we smoked our pipes and drifted off until some hours later we woke to him standing over us, frowning at the timepiece in his hand. Then he looked up and his face burst with a big generous smile. 'Boys,' he said. 'Welcome to 1906.'

*

New Year's Day we breakfasted in bed, spoke a pissabout Maori/*franglais* and used up all our 'mercis' and 'beaucoups' to organise a pot of tea since none of us drank 'café'.

Midday we dragged ourselves from bed, shaved, and packed our boots for the car ride out to Parc des Princes. A car ride! It was the second time we'd driven to the park on match day.

It was bitterly cold but a crowd of 12,000 turned up with their white kerchiefs and black umbrellas. Whoever was fit to play pulled on the jersey:

		Booth		
Harper		Wallace		Abbott
	Mynott		Hunter	
		Stead		
	Gallaher			
	Mackrell		Tyler	
Glasgow		Newton	Cunningham	
	Seeling		Glenn	

The Colour of Distance

The French front row sported beards and as far away as wing and fullback the helpless giggling of our front rowers could be heard.

The ground was a gravel pitch with very little turf.

Bunny Abbott started the scoring. Then the French scored. Bravo! Bravo! We were happy for them. Yes. Cessieux dived over for France and 12,000 umbrellas were thrown in the air. 'Le brave! Cessieux, Cessieux! Un essai, un essai!' The French players did handsprings and hugged one another. We grinned like lizards. Dave Gallaher passed the word round to let the French score again.

The French forwards took play into our quarter, whereupon our backs wandered out of position or looked up at the Parisien skies to help Jerome find space. 'Just before the line he stopped and looked back to make certain the whistle hadn't blown, then dived over.' Again, umbrellas went up around the ground. Waiting on the conversion Dave said, 'That'll do them,' and we set about collecting six tries ourselves.

*

We liked the French
We were surprised to discover that we liked the French
We had an inkling that we were not supposed to

*

In Paris—how we liked saying that—
In Paris we visited the sights:
acted the goat along the Champs-Elysées
put a scrum down before the Arc de Triomphe
wandered the halls of Versailles
explored the Grand Trianon, the palace
Louis XIV built for his mistress.
We marvelled that a private affair
could materialise

Lloyd Jones

73

into such a monumental thing.

Here, in the Tuileries, you saw how trees grew
wanting to do their best.
You saw spires
and understood that where thoughts went to
was exactly the same place where ideas were fetched down.

In Paris, we let our eyes wander the fabled skyline.

In Paris, the clouds moved sedately
like debutantes
very aware, we felt, of where they were
as we were.

In Paree—how we liked saying that—in Paree, we saw our
own ideas promoted in art. In England we were celebrated
for never producing the same move twice in a match, while
in Paree we saw the same idea magnificently expressed in the
stained glass window of Sainte-Chapelle where no two panels
of glass are alike.

In Paris, we went our different ways—
The loosies went off with O'Sullivan
to soak up the atmosphere
of Place de la Concorde
where the heads of aristocrats had rolled.

A man from Cooks, a scholar of Latin and antiquities
escorted Billy Stead to see the 'green woman' by Matisse
& the Venus de Milo
in the afternoon Billy sat at Emile Zola's desk
picturing the Aegean filled with sailing vessels
their decks crammed with statues—Zeus, Hermes, Apollo
roped to a mast, Diana playing her harp on the bow of an
Albanian schooner.

History. It felt good to work yourself into that old story.

Jenny Bornholdt

While the 2002 Meridian Energy Katherine Mansfield Memorial Fellow, Jenny Bornholdt (born 1960) wrote 'Ode to the Little Hotel'. The poem, accompanied by a suite of drawings by Gregory O'Brien, was posted back to New Zealand and hand-printed, concertina-format, by Brendan O'Brien (the production can be viewed at http://www.nzepc.auckland.ac.nz/authors/bornholdt). Various copies were, in due course, distributed along the Côte d'Azur. The poem was subsequently included in *Summer* (2003).

Ode to the Little Hotel

Little Hotel
we love you
and in your little
rooftop room we love
each other, even though
we are big
and hardly worthy of such
a little bed.

We love the street
you stand on
which is neither long
nor short, but somewhere
in between. And we love
your neighbours
who are our friends—
smaller than us
and so ideally suited
to their address.

O Little Hotel we love
your breakfast room
your petit déjeuner
the crypt we reach by
steep narrow stairs
a bob and curtsy on the last
to miss the bottom
beam—we love
all this.

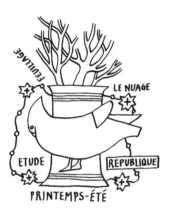

You are our first
and last of Paris, Little
Hotel. We love
your lightning and the
rinsing rain, the way
your white towels sound
the slap of surf
outside our room.

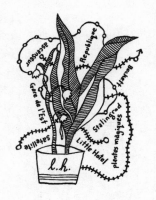

You are the rabbit
of Paris. The duck
with beans and peas.
Little Hotel you are
our herb and cheese,
our soup and sauce,
you are all of these.

O Little Hotel
we love your lift
in which we are
always pleased
to know each
other, pressed so close
as we are.
And when we take them
we love your stairs—
wide enough for one
winding up to light.

Jenny Bornholdt   77

Little Hotel
your windows through which
we duck and climb
to stand on your roof
and look out over
other roofs, we hold these
dear to us.

You are paint and wood
and stone and all things made
from these. O Little Hotel
you are a gallery
of leaves.

You are our pink suit
of Paris, Little Hotel, our men
in shorts, our jazz band.
Later we will slap our knees
and remember you as four musicians
outside the Sorbonne.

The Colour of Distance

O Little Hotel
in whose room
we read and
rest a little
after long days
we revere you.

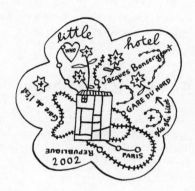

O Little Hotel
we will never
forget you. We will write
and we will return.
O Little Hotel
doorway to our city
of Paris
au revoir.

Jenny Bornholdt

Bill Culbert

Born in Port Chalmers in 1935, Bill Culbert left New Zealand in 1957, at the same time as John Drawbridge, both recipients of New Zealand Art Societies Fellowships to study in London and obtain what was considered at the time a serious art education. Within a few years Culbert had gained a teaching appointment at the Royal College of Art and had purchased on an old farmhouse in an obscure corner of Provence. In recent years Culbert has divided his time chiefly between London and Provence, with annual excursions back to New Zealand, where he exhibits regularly and has undertaken public sculpture commissions. Recent photographic work appears in the Dunedin Public Art Gallery publication *light wine things: Bill Culbert* (2005). These photographs, spanning three decades of his work, alternate between his adopted home in Provence and his birthplace beside Otago Harbour.

Croagnes/Port Chalmers

Carey's Bay, 1978
Jug, Croagnes, 1980
Taiaroa Heads, 1992
Light box, 1989
Port Chalmers, 1978
Small glass pouring light, 1997
Blueskin Bay, 1992
Trousers, Contadour, 1981

Dylan Horrocks

Dylan Horrocks (born 1966) is New Zealand's leading comic writer/artist. His graphic novel *Hicksville* was first published in 1998 and has been translated into several languages, including French. He has recently quit writing the monthly *Batgirl* for DC Comics, to concentrate on new graphic novel projects, including *Atlas* and *Venus: the Secret Comics of Arthur Holly*.

Coming Home

I used to have a drawing by American gag cartoonist B. Kliban on my wall: a man is walking down a city street, wearing a flash suit, cravat and dark glasses, cane in one hand. On each arm a scantily clad woman simpers. Ahead of him, a policeman is pushing a blind pencil seller off the pavement, growling: 'Out of the way, swine! A cartoonist is coming!'

I was reminded of this cartoon on a crisp January evening in 2002, when my wife and I attended the Angoulême comics festival in southern France. A group of us were preparing to leave the CNBDI (a huge, publicly-funded comics museum), when two *gendarmes* (armed with machine guns) suddenly appeared on the footpath. They had seen the badges identifying us as invited guests—*cartoonists*—and, with a brisk nod and a wave of their hands, they stepped out into the middle of the busy street and brought the traffic to a halt. For the cartoonists to cross the road.

Growing up in New Zealand, most people I knew considered comics little more than sub-literate trash—on a par with bubblegum wrappers or the jokes that come in Christmas crackers. The two exceptions—found in every school and public library and loved by all—were *Asterix* and *Tintin*. In fact, most people didn't even think of these hardbound books as comics, but I knew better. As a fanboy, I also knew where they were from: those distant, enchanted lands where people speak *French!*

Without a doubt, Hergé's *Tintin* was my favourite—and the main reason I chose to become a cartoonist. These were comics as novels, and good ones too. Rich and complex characters, intricate, fully-realised plots and subtle, intelligent

81

themes—not to mention the beautiful drawings! *That's* what I will do with my life, I decided. I will make books like *these*.

Of course *Tintin* is Belgian. But he spoke French, and was so popular in France that Charles de Gaulle once described him as '*mon seul rival international*'. And *Tintin* is the main reason I learnt French. There's one *Tintin* book, *On a marché sur la lune*, which we only had in the French edition. I remember lying in bed staring at those cryptic speech balloons, while my father translated them for my sister and me. Right there and then, I think, I learned the magic of knowing another language. Because anything that could give you access to so sweet a treasure as *Tintin* was worth it.

So I studied French right through school, from Form One to Seven. Not that all those long years of memorising vocabulary and struggling with tenses prepared me for the task of checking the French translation of my first graphic novel, *Hicksville*. In short, there's no easy way to translate 'fuck' into French; '*merde*' just doesn't carry the same bundle of connotations, but in the end we were stuck with it.

The best thing about my book coming out in France, though, was being invited to that amazing festival in Angoulême—'The Cannes of comics', as it's known. I'd been before, as a wide-eyed small-press cartoonist. But this time I was '*un dessinateur invité*', and—well, that was something else.

It started the moment we got off the train. I asked at the information desk if there was a bus going up to the festival headquarters. The woman there eyed me curiously and asked my name. 'Ah, Monsieur Horrocks,' she exclaimed, 'I will summon a car!' And for the rest of the weekend that's how it went. All my wife or I had to do was ask someone official how to get somewhere and they would 'summon a car'! And unlike American comics conventions (which are loud, aggressively commercial sales fairs), Angoulême is more like an art festival—organised around well-attended panel discussions, an endless round of exhibition openings, author signings and, of course, the annual *Prix Alph-Art* ceremony.

Now, the Anglophone comics scene has its awards, too. America's Eisners, Harveys and Ignatz Awards, Britain's Eagles, and even New Zealand's humble Erics. But no one outside the comics ghetto has even heard of those. As I said, France is different. The first time I attended the *Alph-Art* ceremony (in 1991), the whole thing was nationally televised. In 2002, two things struck me about the event: first, the big winner on the night was Marjane Satrapi's *Persepolis*, a beautiful and simply-drawn autobiographical account of growing up in Iran, published by a small artists' cooperative. And second, Satrapi was mobbed by the media the moment the ceremony ended. And I mean *mobbed*. There were TV news crews, radio journalists, press photographers—all clamouring for her attention. Satrapi was a *bona fide* media event.

After the festival, we took a train south to Carcassonne (where every bookstore had the *Alph-Art* winners displayed in the window). On the way I glanced through the daily newspapers and found to my amazement that the weekend's events at Angoulême were front page news. 'Grand Prix for Schuiten!' the headlines screamed. Page after page of interviews with cartoonists, analysis of new publishing trends and photos of the unveiling of a statue of Hergé in front of the Angoulême town hall. Apparently, this isn't unusual. Every year the festival is marked by a couple of the major dailies with a magazine-sized supplement. And when the grand old man himself, Hergé, died in 1982, *Libération*'s front page bore a striking image of Snowy (or *Milou* as he's called in the original) wailing over his fallen master, below the words *'Tintin est mort'*. Inside, every news story was illustrated not with a photograph but with a panel from *Tintin*. Every time I think about that extraordinary tribute by one of France's major newspapers, I get all choked up. Because, to a cartoonist from New Zealand, that level of respect and enthusiasm for the humble medium of comics is inconceivable.

Hicksville, the book that earned me a ticket to Angoulême, imagines a small town on the East Cape where comics are king. The local book exchange has copies of every comic published anywhere in the world. In the tearooms, sheep farmers discuss their favourite early newspaper strips and pore over the latest mini-comics from Finland. It was my attempt to create an imaginary *turangawaewae*, or spiritual homeland, for the global community of people who love comics.

Which is why, as we stepped out into that clear wintry evening in Angoulême, while two *gendarmes* brought the traffic to a halt, I felt like I'd come home.

Dylan Horrocks   83

À Cornucopia, elle m'avait dit que son jardin était le seul repère qui lui restait. Parfois elle regardait même par-dessus son épaule, presque sûre de le voir là, à l'attendre.

Georgia O'Keefe
ive, New York Museum of Modern Art. Aug 1-Oct 25

Elle travaillait à l'institut botanique de Crieste, et elle croisait souvent des plantes qu'elle avait rencontrées dans son jardin, comme autant de lettres de chez elle.

J'ai toujours considéré les plantes comme un simple élément du paysage, une partie d'un lieu. Mais pour Grace, elles habitaient le lieu, tout comme nous. Beaucoup étaient des nomades, conquérant ici et continuant plus loin. Pour elle, son jardin était une communauté, un sanctuaire.

Elle m'a dit que c'était pour lui qu'elle était revenue. Juste pour le jardin.

Et maintenant il était désespérément détruit, elle le reconnaissait à peine. Les mauvaises herbes avaient tout colonisé, étouffant et dépossédant tout le reste. Irrécupérablement.

Ce n'était plus son paysage. C'était comme un exil.

Bill Manhire

While Meridian Energy Katherine Mansfield Memorial Fellow in 2004, Bill Manhire (born 1946) traveled to Alzon—a small French town located at exactly the opposite point on the globe to the Chatham Islands. There he was caught up in a civic event: a rugby match between locals and New Zealanders. Manhire's poems from this time are included in *Lifted* (2005).

Song: Alzon

Alzon hides behind itself.
It talks in Occitan.
The stars above Alzon.
The water beside Alzon.

There is one song,
then always another song.
The pines of the night.
The words of this poem.

He loves her but . . . the way
lies through that tunnel
and across the difficult bridge
by which one enters Le Vigan.

So many people!
Everything is wrong.

The hidden paths.
The tunnelling paths.
Alzon hides behind itself.
It talks in Occitan.

86

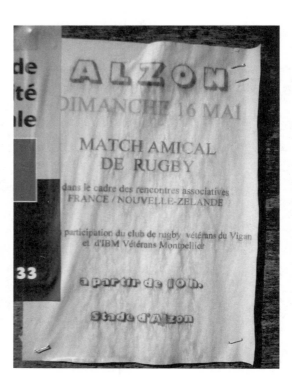

Part Two

The French
in New Zealand

Vincent O'Sullivan

Novelist, playwright, poet, biographer and critic, Vincent O'Sullivan (born 1937) was Katherine Mansfield Memorial Fellow in Menton in 1994. In 1990 he was commissioned to write a one-actor piece to be performed at the French Colloquium at Akaroa on 17 August. Written in English, the monologue was translated into French by Christiane Mortelier and performed by Bruce Phillips. O'Sullivan notes: 'The piece opens with the first four lines of Baudelaire's "L'Homme et la Mer". The lines "Regardez en cette visage" are adapted from those engraved on a portrait of Meryon by Felix Braquemond. Other verse quotations are—with occasional slight changes—from Meryon himself.'

O'Sullivan's subject, Charles Meryon (1821–68), spent two years in the French navy, based at Akaroa, before returning to Paris, where he became a renowned etcher before being committed to a mental institution.

Qui êtes-vous vraiment Monsieur Meryon?

Homme libre, toujours tu chériras la mer!
La mer est ton miroir, tu contemples ton âme
Dans le déroulement infini de sa lame,
Et ton esprit n'est pas un gouffre moins amer.

He wanted—M. Baudelaire—he wanted to write poems for me. For me. Can you imagine that? For the etchings I did of Paris. My famous pictures. 'La Morgue.' 'Le Pont Neuf.' You must have seen them? Must have seen the way I move the shadows and let the paper speak whiter, more pure, as my shadows grow more thick. And always something that puzzles as you look. Why I place birds there wheeling like flakes of soot. Like the streaming of black snow.

Baudelaire said my pictures were visions as well as facts. He said, 'In the cross-hatched lines of your etchings all becomes a dreadful mirror. I am the only poet who understands these things.' He was standing right there, in my studio, when he said he wanted to find the words that would match what I saw. He said, 'I too am an explorer of the modern soul. I have images that equal yours.' His forests of ships' masts and the musk of black women he cannot resist with hair like wet heavy ropes. M. Baudelaire standing here, at my shoulder, as he watches my blade move slowly across the metal plates. He said, 'You use your knife like a surgeon, you are a true artiste.' And I said to him, 'M. Baudelaire, I will find my own words for my own scored flesh. You are a great poet but I do not need you. I am who I am.'

'Ah,' he said, 'but who are you *exactly*, Charles Meryon?'

You must let me tell you then, a little. It was not always tin plates I ate from. Locked doors. This beard which makes me look like a madman, no? Even you, M. Baudelaire, do not know everything about the soul. You do not know how innocence corrupts more profoundly than those favourite words of yours—luxury, boredom. There are more frightening things than those. There is space and savagery. There is the nakedness of things exactly as they are.

You must let me go back to before this cell at Charenton. We are not here, for the moment. We are back to when I wore this jacket. Lieutenant, you notice that? When my ship *Le Rhin* rode at anchor not two hundred metres from where you are sitting now. Akaroa. 'The long harbour.' I could not believe it when we sailed through the black cliffs into this calm. The forest grew to the water's edge. In the mornings we stood on deck and the sound of birds was beyond belief. The natives moved on the shoreline like figures in ancient stories, like turning a Greek vase. Oh, we were full of Rousseau in those days! Full of humanity. Optimism. I had never seen such men, such women, as in Tahiti. I remembered our Revolution was for them as much as us—remember the slogans? 'Liberty for all races, all men as brothers.' To be French was to carry that torch. The first race of Europe hand in hand with the noble savage. You see this friend I drew in Akaroa? Ah well. Our dreams founder on the reefs of fact. Where I wanted my savages to be gods I saw poverty and laziness and dirt. For the torch of equality we shared with them the flare of disease. *Reads from letter*: 'Le contact des Européens là, comme partout, ne leur est que défavorable; ils se corrompent au lieu

92   *The Colour of Distance*

de s'améliorer et chaque jour marchent à leur perte.'

Yet I am still a young man. When I ask myself what should life be, I want the world to answer—it will be what you make it. Sin is not our destiny. To be a bastard is not a flaw across existence. This man I write to—mon père—an English doctor. My mother is a dancing girl at the Paris opera and will die insane at thirty-eight. My birth is a small black bird that flies above me, very high, on even the finest days. I look at Mt Benoit across the harbour there—that lovely peak, you know it? Above the bush, above our little inconsequential port. There is a circling hawk beside that high pure rock. I understand such things.

I am here for two years. I draw pictures. We sail to other islands. To Valparaiso. Sydney. I walk these hills until I know them better than I do anywhere on earth. I grow into the Pacific until I seem another man. And then I return home. 'Oh, le beau et bon pays que la France, comme on apprend à l'aimer quand on est éloigné!' You cannot imagine Paris in the 1840s. Before the world turned sour. When the future of man still seemed a broad path to freedom. I thought myself the very man to draw that path. Let me tell you about one picture I had planned. 1848, the year of light! A square picture. A triangular group, apex slightly to the right, the horizon lit up to the left. France is the principal figure and rises from a heap of ruins, the mirror of truth held high in her right hand. A naked boy child is at her side. In the foreground a girl binds the wounds of a victorious but dying warrior. The picture was still in my mind when the barricades fell, when the monarchy was restored, when the people of Paris were crushed, and so it was never done. The noble European is no more true then than the noble savage. Under cannibalism man eats man. Under capitalism the reverse is true. So much for Hope!

Ton esquif passager sur l'orageuse mer
Qu'on appelle la Vie, Océan dur, amer,
Ou trop souvent, hélas, fallacieux rivage,
L'esprit qui nous leurrait va mourir au rivage.

There was a girl in a restaurant who was supposed to have driven me mad. It says so in the books. She was a waitress in a cheap establishment and my disappointment brought me to this. To have made me an isolato. Listen to this. 'The lonely meditations of a brain already morbid, suspicious in later life and shrinking from human intercourse, were visible even then in his melancholy.' I am not interested in temperament, my dear friends. God has chosen me for more than temperament! He has chosen me for truth. *Looks at himself in mirror.*

Regardez en cette image
Le sombre Meryon
Au grotesque visage.

A man tells the truth by looking at things exactly as they are. Yet that is very hard. Because there is perspective, which speaks to us in different voices. There is the curve of a stone, say, the solidness of a wall with sunlight falling across it. They remain exact. Precise. They also change while I walk. Every artist, you see, must tell two truths at the same time. The world is there, like this hand. The world is disappearing, as my hand also disappears . . . two, one, nada. . . . Let me tell you about the divine lie which is art.

You will know my etching 'Le Petit Pont'? A row of austere buildings above the Quai, the towers of Notre Dame above the buildings. It is very famous. And the towers in fact are higher than the laws of perspective allow—the *idea* of Notre Dame, you see, as well as every inch of it, to perfection. This is what I do. I make a drawing from down here, near the edge of the river. I am looking directly up—so. Then I draw it again, from here, as every passer-by will see it. I then fit both together to make my etching. I do not copy Notre Dame, you notice. I *compose* it with an accuracy more piquant than any sighting can ever do. Every detail—a ledge as delicate as frost, the grand elegant pilasters—these are there with more precision than any eye before mine has ever noticed. They are also there as no other eye shall ever see them again, except through me.

My line, then, which is so respected for its truth, is an instrument to carry us past mere fact. It lets the spirit talk

The Colour of Distance

to me from stone. And what do you think the spirit of Paris is? Imagine, to begin with, that you look through these walls towards the hills. You see the snagged fleeces of the clouds on those majestic rocks. You see a southern ocean more pure than we conceive. You see the natives at ease with Original Sin. They have neither the need nor the desire to make themselves children of God. And now imagine everything that you mean by that word European. You dip that word in the Pacific and it breaks up like sodden bread. The feast of civilisation becomes an empty plate. You see what we have to fear. And always the paradox, my friends. The beauty of a face like this. *Indicates drawing of a Maori head*. And here are we. *Turns to drawing of Le Stryge, the gargoyle on Notre Dame*. Which is the face that tells me more of Christ? And which is the history of what we are? The story of the streets we walk in every day? Ah, M. Baudelaire, I have my own poems too. I have words for our friend here. Notre image. Notre semblable!

Insatiable vampire, l'eternelle luxure
Sur la grande cité convoite sa pâture.

I am not always this solemn, of course! Sometimes I put balloons in the sky over Paris. I call one Speranza. I call another Vasco de Gama. My friends simply don't know what to say. Whoever saw that kind of armada over Paris? I did, I say. And sometimes I see canoes and whales where others only see a drifting cloud. Ah Charles, they say, what a sense of the bizarre! And I tell them other secrets I know. I say if we gave up this lecherous indulgent notion of sleeping on beds level as this table. If we gave up that, I tell them, if we slept on an angle like this, facing the rising sun, would not our lives make so much more sense? I have done it myself. A couple of long boards. Ropes round here to keep you from falling down. There is such an effort in sleeping, the mind has no time for sensual thoughts! But tell people this and how embarrassed they become! Or we are walking along the street, say, and someone says there is a good place to eat down here, it is only a few minutes. No, I say. But they say it's very good. So I tell them how in every doorway in that street there is a

Jesuit observing us. The enemies of progress and liberty in every doorway, in their silent black slippers and their Spanish cloaks. At first they think this too is a joke. How can you know such things, Meryon? How do I know the sun shines, I say? How do I know the rain makes me wet? You might as well ask me to doubt that I breathe. Or to believe it is not wrong to eat while others go hungry. You see this arm, for instance? When I was an officer in New Zealand it was as thick as that. When I ate pork and drank wine with every meal. When I was a young man and simply didn't think. And the poor in Paris, in those days? The poor were everywhere, and like the poor at all times, they were hungry. And now I look at my meagre arm and know that things are so much better for them. I am hungry nearly always, but there are not so many poor. Slowly, slowly, I turn my empty plate into a shining world. I see such things in Paris you must promise not to tell.

'Le Collège Henri IV', you must all know that? My picture that will puzzle the future more than any other. At first it is a panorama. There is the great rectangle of the College itself, the high buildings that surround the courtyards. Next to those, on the right, the formal gardens, then further right again, the rows of houses. On the side of one house you might see my monogram—so elaborately drawn that in the distance it is like an eye. In the foreground there are naked classical figures, so much larger than life. They are the figures we Europeans revere—but they too are confused and afraid. And why not? At the back of the etching, at the end of our city streets, there is already the Ocean. There is the promise of deluge. And you will see not only the Ocean. You will see a small figure is riding a whale. There are the triangular canvasses of Polynesian canoes. Is it not so very clear? Paris between its antique dreams, its civilisation, and the rising tide of empire, of a damaged world, corroding its margins.

I draw this picture over again. It is the same view of almost the same things. Only you notice now the water is higher, the streets are in flood. The naked figures are wading for their lives. For you see how the Ocean from those outskirts has poured across the city. The canoes are larger. Leviathan is riding to his new home. This is the conscience of France turning on itself.

And you notice where the city and the invading Ocean meet? That house that breaks the engulfing tide? It is the home of Charles Meryon who is both Paris and the flood.

You will understand then Victor Hugo. You know what that great man said of me? Of this mind that the doctors tell you is corrupting into chaos? 'Cette belle imagination', that is what he called it. 'Il ne faut pas que cette belle imagination soit châtiée de la grande lutte qu'elle livre à l'infini, tantôt en contemplant l'Océan, tantôt en contemplant Paris.' My mind which is at the border of immense terror, immense calm. What I offer you, mes chers confrères, is that indecision in yourself. To see the dreadful accuracy of things exactly as they are. To know the wheeling, riding visions above the streets we walk. To guess the shadows of each doorway as we pass. Oh, there is nothing to sharpen one's pencil like being a bastard, when it is human folly one wants to draw!

Quel mortel habitait
En ce gîte si sombre?
Qui donc la se cachait,
Dans la nuit et dans l'ombre;

Etait-ce la Vertu,
Pauvre silencieuse?
Le crime, diras-tu,
Quelqu'âme vicieuse.

Ah! ma foi, je l'ignore;
Si tu veux le savoir,
Curieux, vas-y voir
Il en est temps encore.

Il en est temps toujours . . . This gift of perception the medical profession presumes to call my 'delirious melancholia'. As though to be a little more than sane disturbs these mere doctors, these mechanics of the body. Even my death you will find documented as a kind of dementia. You will read that on 14 February 1868, believing myself Christ detained by the Pharisees, I continue in my refusal to deprive the poor of their food. Yet ask yourselves. Is a man to be called demented who starves himself for his friends? Such a man is very certain, indeed. Very deliberate. And the brave are always sane—a fact which unsettles the ordinary mind extraordinarily! . . . Well, we have seen a great deal together, you and I. The Akaroa you see almost as clearly as I did from Charenton. The waves. Always the waves. Mt Benoit. Mt Herbert. You cannot look at these hills, this harbour, these circling birds, with more care than I have given them. You cannot look at our world, look at each other, with more disillusionment, yet with more love.

J'espère en un autre âge,
Naviguant dans tes yeux,
Revoir encore la plage,
La mer et les vaissaux.

Mon ami et matelot,
Humanité, toi que j'aime
Comme un autre moi-même,
A revoir, à bientôt!

Charles Meryon, *Le Collège Henri IV*, 1864

The Colour of Distance

Blaise Cendrars

introduced by Michael Jackson

It was Henry Miller's *The Books in My Life* that introduced me to Blaise Cendrars, though it was a Swiss cabinet-maker whose name I have forgotten who put into my hands a Livre de Poche edition of Cendrars' *Bourlinguer,* which I read, appropriately, on board ship between Sydney and Genoa in 1963. However, it was *Moravagine,* which I bought in Paris a couple of months later and re-read in the Congo in 1964, that really blew me away. Here was a man after my own heart—a poet of the new modernity who was also drawn to the margins of the modern world, broke with literary conventions and exemplified the truth of Gertrude Stein's wonderful phrase, 'What good are your roots if you can't take them with you.' Over the next few years I translated large chunks of Cendrars's prose and poetry, and imitated his style in my own essays at prose-fiction. Few other writers have had such an impact on me, and I still draw inspiration from Cendrars's determination to make literature do justice to life, 'to prove that a novel can also be an act'. Numerous excerpts from Cendrars's writings appear in my forthcoming memoir, *The Accidental Anthropologist,* but the first translation I published was of his 'Noël en Nouvelle-Zélande' (from *Trop c'est trop,* Denoël, Paris, 1957, pp. 109–12), in which Cendrars recalls a sojourn in New Zealand in the 1920s (*Comment* 25, pp. 35–6). Though Cendrars' memory may have played him false (the Australian shark-nets and eucalypts for instance), it is his idyllic picture of New Zealand that strikes me as the real anomaly, for not only does Cendrars eulogise the kind of pastoral environments and domesticity that he fled as a fifteen-year-old boy, vowing never to return; he overlooks the violent history of dispossession that lay behind New Zealand's deforested hills and pioneer farms.

The collected poems of Blaise Cendrars, translated by Ron Padgett, appeared in 1992. Born in the Swiss town of Les-Chaux-de-Fonds in 1887, Cendrars settled in Paris in 1910. Travelling widely, he spent his life as a soldier, film-maker, merchant seaman, journalist and essayist. He later became a French citizen, although tended to think of himself primarily as a 'citizen of the world'.

Christmas in New Zealand

In the antipodes. The austral summer. It's Christmas. I've got down off my horse, and from the top of a dune can see the crowded beach, city people frolicking behind the shark nets. The whale-shark has three rows of teeth and six thousand teeth in each of its jaws. Yesterday, it was a troupe of seals basking in the sun; the day before two pairs of sea elephants disporting offshore. I tie up my horse and go down for a swim, then get dressed, leap in the saddle, make a half turn, and head straight inland. It's Christmas. The shepherds. The star. The manger. The blue angels of Piombino in the Vatican sacristy. The music of the spheres. *Peace on earth, goodwill to all men* . . . Sheep. The other year, I was in Rome . . .

If there is a Land of Milk and Honey anywhere on this earth it is, at first sight, New Zealand. On these two isles of the blessed, pedigree herds and flocks graze the lush grass of deep valleys. From one year to another, nothing disturbs them. You can travel by car for days, or on horseback for weeks, and never meet a living soul. You can cross ridges, descend into untracked valleys, and never leave these pasturelands. Except for a petrified waterfall, a wild spot decked out in Swiss miniature and reserved for newlyweds looking for a place to honeymoon or retired couples celebrating a golden anniversary, or some groves of tropical plants—as exotic, rare, and hardy as those in Ceylon, especially the great cruciform tree ferns which are all that remain of the primitive flora of the country—nothing picturesque meets the eye. The entire interior is divided into rectangles by high, five-stranded barbed wire fences that separate the paddocks. Valley succeeds valley in soft succession with nothing to interrupt the sameness and monotony of the glistening grassland that spreads everywhere, indelibly green, reflecting the sky as does a sheet of water, invading the landscape, pervading it with quietness, stillness, peace, and warm silence.

With a bit of luck, you may happen upon a stand of tall eucalypts in whose pungent shadows, filled with the cooing of turtle doves and the rustling of papery leaves, you will find a farm, if you can call it a farm—this spanking new bungalow where a settler who is not a 'peasant' and his lady who is not a 'farmer's wife', sit of an evening at their pianola or lean forward listening to the wireless.

Night was falling. The night of Christmas Eve. I had been riding through the backblocks all day and was completely lost. But I rode on into the star-filled night, disoriented less by the stunning brightness of the Southern Cross than by the millions of flickering lights from the frantic fireflies.

Finally, I dismounted in a grove of trees. Tied my horse to a tree. The eucalypts balmy. A wan light visible between the trunks of the paperbarks and snatches of music betraying the position of a farmhouse at the head of the valley. A piano playing.

I approached the house without a sound, and have never forgotten the astonishing sight that met my eyes: a man and a woman, he in a smoking jacket, she in a *décolletée* evening gown with a string of pearls around her neck. They were sitting side by side on an upholstered stool, their backs to the open window, and playing the piano with three hands. The piece was *Pagliacci*. Behind them, on a table, an oil lamp, a plum pudding in a tin water-bath on a Primus stove, a bottle of whisky, some glasses . . . I stood there for a long while despite the tiredness that had come over me, watching these two people playing solely for each other, shoulder to shoulder, smiling radiantly. They were alone on the face of the earth . . .

At midnight I introduced myself. They didn't tell me their story. Maybe they didn't have one. They were a happy couple and had chosen to be alone. It's a priceless secret . . . peace . . . contentment . . . But no one passes an entire lifetime in such complete isolation, and the man had been in the war and, like me, lost an arm there . . .

Strange meeting. But that Christmas Eve was a good one. He with his right, I with my left, drinking together.

An Anzac from the Artois.

My God, how small the world is when one travels!

Denis Lalanne

and the 1961 French Rugby Tour of New Zealand

The 1961 tour by the French national side to what T. P. McLean called 'the land of the long white goalposts' came at a time of unprecedented prestige for French rugby. The team had recently won the Five Nations championship and held the Springboks to a scoreless draw in Paris.

The Tricolours' antipodean tour was the subject of one of the classic pieces of extended rugby journalism, Denis Lalanne's *La Mêlée Fantastique* (1962), which was translated into English by Edwin Boyd-Wilson, a retired Victoria University College professor of modern languages, who acted as official interpreter for the French team.

The mainstay of New Zealand rugby journalism at that time, T. P. McLean wrote his own account of the tour: a 'rugby entertainment' entitled *Cock of the Rugby Roost* (Reed, 1961), which included thumbnail summations of each of the French players:

> JEAN DUPUY, a mad wag of a humorist and a good singer, wore a reputation as the greatest wing in French history as easily as he wore a blond moustache, tinged with ginger, which vaguely recalled the adornment of that celebrated character of the screen, Dr Fu Manchu. The moustache was always present. Unfortunately, Dupuy was not . . .
>
> PIERRE ALBALADEJO had his name mispronounced more times than any ten Tricolours put together . . . The crowd at Eden Park for the First Test with the All Blacks showed signs of a-sighing and a-sobbing too, when 'M'sieu le Drop' bowled a couple of beauties over the bar in the first half, but like an artist who becomes entranced with the products of his own imagination, Pierre afterwards restricted his view of the world to the drop and almost nothing but the drop.
>
> JEAN-PIERRE SAUX wore rimless spectacles, he read books of a serious character, he bore himself with a detached, even remote and always kindly air . . .
>
> PIERRE LACROIX . . . On the morning of a match, Lacroix was the leader of a small group which lunched, in the highest style, at 9.15 in the morning. The wine would be there, the rare steak, the salad and the conversation—but always, and first and foremost, the conversation. An hour, perhaps an hour and a half later, the ceremonial rite would come to an end and there would be no more food until after the match.

In such a fashion, McLean made his way through the entire touring party, making, one can only imagine, a number of enemies as well as friends along the way.

Having published *The Great Fight of the French Fifteen* ('Le grand combat du quinze de France'), Denis Lalanne was considered one of the world's outstanding sports journalists. A highlight of his account of the New Zealand tour is the description of the second test match in the capital. Having lost against the All Blacks in Auckland, and with only one further test to play after the Wellington confrontation, the French desperately needed a win to stay in the series. Lalanne evokes the mood at Athletic Park on the big day. The weather was so appalling he was reminded of the Book of Revelations. (T. P. McLean later wrote unequivocally that the game should have been cancelled: 'The New Zealand Rugby Union, as the host, was very grievously at fault in directing that it should go on.') Lalanne, believing all things equal in rugby, took a more stoic approach:

> Now, in that static war, in that hell on earth in which sixteen
> forwards faced one another and were soon exhausted, the
> French have this to their great credit: they fought as well
> and used the same weapons as the All Blacks, because in the
> hurricane there was nothing for it but to push in the scrum, to
> wheel the scrum, to pick themselves up and hurl themselves
> into the scrum.

The All Blacks scraped to a 5 points to 3 victory (and, accordingly, won the three-test-match series). Lalanne writes, with a mixture of Gallic passion and despair, about the embattled first half which left the French, as well as the All Blacks, scoreless despite the fact the visitors had the gale blowing behind them.

from **La Mêlée Fantastique**

**For Whom the Wind Blows;
New Zealand—Second Test**

I shall always remember how, on the morning of this historic test match, on 5 August, I received a cable from my editor-in-chief in Paris. It contained instructions for the transmission of my next cablegram and ended with this message for the Equipe de France:

'Favourable winds.'

Denis Lalanne   103

Well, as for the wind, no one will ever forget the storm, the hurricane, if it was not a cyclone, which arose a few hours before the kickoff, with a fury which defies description. It was a hellish uproar, a cataclysm like the crack of doom. Its first moanings reached us in the night. In the morning it was ravaging Wellington, howling at sixty-five miles an hour; it was frightening people and driving the *Canberra* back two miles outside the harbour.

Play Rugby in such conditions?

'Why not a test match on top of Mont Blanc?' suggested Andy Mulligan.

But an H-bomb exploding on the halfway line would not stop New Zealanders from kicking off at the appointed time— and this match would put on record the All Blacks' ultimate triumph or the Tricolours' last chance.

Taking refuge in one of the lounges, pierced to the marrow by the turbine-like whistling of the hurricane, the boys were leaving it in the hands of fate, but at the same time they were grimly summoning up all their energy. Marcel Laurent asked those who weren't playing to leave him alone with the chosen fifteen for a last team talk, which only added to the uneasiness they all felt. Then came the moment to leave for Athletic Park. When we reached the dressing-room door, Domenech cried out, as he swung his leather headgear about:

'Farewell, boys, I am about to die!'

The ground was a nightmare spectacle. Entrance to sections of the giddy stand recently erected was forbidden, because of the risk of accident. The spectators, dressed like trampers, formed lines, like mountain climbers roped together, so that they could force their way against the wind and reach their seats. Nylon raincoats flew off and crossed the ground at a height of thirty yards like mad kites. The goalposts shook like ridiculous cornstalks and the corner flags, though firmly set in the ground, were bent almost flat. In this desolate, cyclone-swept stadium, half the seats were empty; for planes, cars and ships had been unable to reach Wellington. It was pitiful, and at the same time wonderful, that the most important game in a Rugby epoch was to take place in this hell let loose, fit only for the sport of demons. We shivered in our seats as we waited for this unparalleled encounter, measurable only in the terms of dread and terror.

Five minutes before the kickoff, a New Zealand colleague ran excitedly into the bay where I was sitting and cried!

'Moncla has won the toss!'

. . .

The players came out on to the ground, bending their backs against the wind, turning aside their heads so as not to be stifled on the spot. The national anthems were dispensed with; they started play as quickly as possible. And it was Moncla himself who caught the crazy ball and with a huge punt sent it from his own 25 down to the other end.

Help! Help! All you writers of fiction and of horror stories give me words to describe this icy encounter, these paralysed lineouts, this stark and stiff Rugby, distorted like a caricature of the devil.

Beneath the murky sky at Athletic Park, in the fantastic whirlwinds, the game rapidly became a series of grotesque and pathetic scenes. It was impossible to throw the ball in from the touchline or even to put it into the scrum. Don Clarke kicked for touch and the ball flew back fifteen yards over his head, right over his own deadball line. Lacroix, behind his scrum, could not at times drop the ball on to his foot to kick it out. A miserable three yards would be gained along the touchline after two prostrate teammates had held the ball in place for the kicker. And all this happened in a tiny perimeter, in the suffocating centre of the hurricane, as it were, into which the ball returned against the players' will: it was a zone of twenty yards at most, along the touchline guarded by Rancoule, who fought on courageously in the midst of his dazed forwards, whose faces grew paler and more gaunt with each succeeding lineout.

Because the All Blacks wanted it that way, the game was reduced to a frightful challenge in the scrums, a slow war of attrition in which the weaker must inevitably perish. Now, in this hell on earth, Whineray's pack at once gave evidence of an overwhelming superiority. His forwards won many tight-heads and especially inflicted on the French forwards the torture of an endless thrust. They held the ball skilfully in the back row and wheeled their scrum to gain five yards along the touchline. But five yards meant a valuable gain of territory and made one wonder how much advantage the Tricolours got from having the wind in their favour. The New Zealand forwards were really giving an impressive performance. The two tall men, MacEwan and Colin Meads, stood out prominently all the time, but for us it was an unbearable sight. The French were killing themselves and, to get a moment's respite from the agonising pushing, were often reduced to getting off-side, which was done by either Crauste or Moncla.

The minutes passed, working for the All Blacks. They were biding their time with cold serenity. They had met the conditions by sending Graham, their wing forward, back in support of Don Clarke, in anticipation of the long kicks which came whirling along in the wind.

By the end of the first spell there was no score. In the sixteenth minute, the wind carried away to the right a kick Albaladejo took from twenty-two yards in front of the posts. Two minutes later an attempted fieldgoal by the same player was charged down by Tremain. In the twenty-second minute, Albaladejo calculated the drift beautifully in an attempt at goal from twenty-two yards, on an angle. But at the last moment a gust sent the ball under the bar. No, there was nothing doing.

When the whistle went for halftime and the teams were given leave to seek shelter in their dressing-rooms, the whole crowd was moved to pity for the little Frenchmen, who certainly were going to be crushed in the second half.

As for us, tears were coming into our eyes. We were filled with secret anger: how stupid to stake such a great reputation against such cursed weather. Let us get out of this country and go back home to play Rugby again. But we stopped cursing and resigned ourselves to watch the inevitable massacre, the horrible death of the French XV.

LA MÉLÉE
FANTASTIQUE

DENIS LALANNE
Author of The Great Fight of the French Fifteen
TRANSLATED BY E. J. BOYD WILSON

THE FRENCH RUGBY TOUR OF NEW ZEALAND 1961

La Mêlée Fantastique (Reed, 1962)

Nadine Ribault

Nadine Ribault lives in the North of France, on the Côte d'Opale, where she writes poetry and fiction. She is the author of a novel, *Festina lente*, and two collections of short stories: *Un caillou à la mer* (published in English translation as *A Pebble into the Sea* by VVV Editions (Canada)), and *Coeur anxieux*, inspired by her time in New Zealand as inaugural Randell Cottage French Fellow in 2002. She was born in Paris, lived for five years in Africa and, more recently, spent five years in Japan.

This story, and the other pieces that are published for the first time in English in this book, were translated by Jean Anderson, who is Senior Lecturer in French at Victoria University.

Breathless

James had propped his crutches against the guard rail. Below it, the sea beat out a terrible cadence, holding nothing back, a huge commotion, a thunderous rushing back and forth against the Pancake Rocks. The basin emptied, filled, was beaten, flayed, filled, emptied, the water pouring in surges from beneath the yellow stone barrier. Down below the fish must be dying from it, the lichen torn to pieces, wrenched from its roots, and the stones were being worn away, century by century, transformed into stacks of pancakes as far as the eye could see. A jet of water shot up from time to time from the Chimney Pot, dissolving into the air in a shower of glittering sparks. The basin emptied. The square-shaped rocks that had fallen by the cave mouth were revealed. Then the sea charged in, its endless attack brutalising Dolomite Point. Cascades and sheets of droplets spilled down the rocky walls and shot out of the pools with a deafening crash. Rivers of water tore themselves open on stony corners and the sea retreated. Watching this demonstration of immense power, the young man felt his heart galloping. It was as if the force that had inhabited him recently was materialising before his very eyes. An energy was flowing from water to stone, identical to the energy that had moved through his body, a few months earlier, allowing him to get himself out of a tricky situation.

'Look!' his wife shouted. 'It's unbelievable!'

The water had just spurted up twice as high. People called out and the children, hoisted up by their parents so they could see, shouted. The visitors were taking photographs and smiling knowingly to one another as they met on the pathway round Punakaiki, drawn together in their shared admiration. Just one little girl in a white dress, her hat askew on her long ringlets, was poking about in the tall grass behind the pathway, paying no attention to the magnificent spectacle.

'Whatever do you mean by that?' his wife had snapped at him the day James had finally dared to ask her if she'd thought of leaving him. 'Marriage is for life and I'm here to help you.'

That was just so typical of her: she had a way of simplifying things. But in spite of this (the sky was grey, lowering, dark) they would never have a little girl in a white dress, or a little boy either.

'And why not?' his wife had asked recently. 'Is there any reason at all why we can't start a family?'

He looked at her, aghast: 'any reason at all . . .'—what about this, then?

'Oh, that!' she exclaimed. 'But you did that on purpose. To test my love for you. And a fat lot of good it did you!'

Through the narrow vertical slits in the rocks James watched the sea, a muddy-looking mass. Patiently, murderously, it beat against the stone basin that emptied, filled, was flayed, filled, emptied, the water pouring in surges from beneath the yellow stone barrier. Here the remains of millions of little dead bodies were piled up against one another, clumped together, colonies of animals, shells and fossilised corals where every shape in fact, thought James, had found a permanent burial place. The sea had such a capacity for change that everything around it had to adapt or be destroyed.

'Come on, get up,' his wife had said one fine morning. 'Get out of bed. You need to have a shower, air out the bedroom. It'll do you good.'

She'd said it several times before, but he hadn't taken it

seriously. He felt sad and weak. He was suffering. How could she promise something like that?

She covered his dressings with plastic bags, sticking them on as best she could with a whole raft of bandaids, while he watched this assemblage in astonishment. How skilful she was, how well she was adapting, never a word of complaint, resourceful, attentive to his every need, morning till night, all night, listening to him, reassuring him, putting her cool hand on his forehead or kissing him gently there.

'Come on,' she said again. 'Get undressed. Oh, now . . . between husband and wife, there's nothing to be embarrassed about. It's bad enough that we're sleeping in separate bedrooms. That would really be the last straw if I can't even give you a hand, wouldn't it?'

She'd laughed.

'So who's my little Quasimodo, then,' she murmured, stroking and tickling him, massaging his knotted (she'd say, a slave's) shoulders and his wrist, where he was starting to get tendinitis.

He'd laughed too then she said . . .

'Let's not get carried away. I'll strip the bed while you have your shower.'

Afterwards he felt faint and his wife had to support him, walking him over to the armchair.

Luckily, although she was slightly built and looked frail, she was pretty tough.

Through the open window the morning sun poured in, harsh, its yellow light flooding over the underblanket on the bed and the pile of sheets thrown on the floor, and while James sat there . . .

'Have you finished?' he kept saying, impatient.

. . . his wife put on fresh sheets, plumped up the pillows then helped him to get back into bed, to settle back into his usual place, the only place where he was able to forget what was now missing: his independence. His life was no longer moving. His spirit, inevitably opened, blossoming in rebellion, had learned to lie down.

His wife closed the window again and he felt better: really, the fresh air, the outdoors, the smell of the flowers were

The Colour of Distance

making him uncomfortable.

'Tomorrow we'll redo your dressings,' she said before she left the room.

She was always planning something.

It took him all morning to recover.

From his bed he could hear his wife moving round the cottage taking care of all the extra tasks she had these days: in the morning, prepare his treatments, change his dressings, the sheets, turn on the washing machine and the dishwasher, clean and scrub the house, make lunch for two; in the afternoon, run by the supermarket, picking out special delicacies to tempt James's appetite (these days, as if in search of strong sensations that might wake him from a dream, he wanted hot peppers, chili con carne, Indian, Thai, African food, things that would burn the lips off you), go to the chemist's, bring back newspapers and x-rays, drop these off at the doctor's office, return his call, and the lab's, fill out the insurance forms (it's so complicated, accidents in the workplace, I've really had enough of it all, she'd say, and it was the only time she lost her patience because that was the least of their problems, she'd say, all these ACC forms now when they had other things to worry about), do the gardening if she had time; and in the evening, cut off and hem the right legs of James's trousers.

'Better not make a mistake, remember it's the right leg,' she'd say for a joke.

She'd always had a quirky sense of humour, strange ideas, secrets, and when she saw the disapproving look on his face . . .

'Such bad taste!' she'd add, rolling her eyes.

Then she had to phone the family, friends, workmates, keep them informed: he didn't want to be endlessly repeating the story, telling them all about the mess he was in, or even listening to them go on about how brave he was.

'They're really concerned about you,' she'd say, and that was the only point when her voice gave her away, her distress showing through, as if, bizarrely, when she felt other people's pity she lost control.

Below him, the water streaming down the rocky walls of the cliffs reminded him of the shower he'd taken that morning.

Nadine Ribault   111

With a breathless gasp, James had felt the water flowing down his legs. He'd looked down and seen, there in the bath-tub, one foot, only one, one leg, only one, short, well-muscled, strong, and, propped against the hand basin like a pair of wings, his crutches.

Like a piece of lichen torn away from the rock, carried off in spite of itself, fighting back up to the surface through the whirlpools, tossing about, panicking, scraping against the smashed bodies of the broken shellfish, James could see himself in the basin, beaten by the sea, carried away on the current, the chaos, the noise, the breath that the sea might give back to him, this breath of the world that flowed inside every living creature, this breath he thought he'd lost just as he thought he'd lost movement, happiness and love—never his zest for life, never!—and he felt himself carried off by a powerful breath of resistance, allowing himself to be taken by the wave and lifted up, somewhere calm, somewhere else, between two stone pancakes, a gap to tuck his new life away in and . . . intoxicated by the sea air and the thunderous racket surrounding him, he straightened up, leaned back suddenly, drenched in sweat, a bitter taste in his mouth, seized with fear, with . . . oh, no, not a damned panic attack!

'Are you coming?' asked his wife, tapping him on the arm and she must have been saying are you coming for a while because she was right beside him, looking up at him, worried.

The dizziness lifted and, stunned to see his wife so upset, he felt his body tensing at once like a bird's. Drunk with a sense of risk like in the old days (in the days when he hoped perhaps that nothing would make him fall or that he'd be able to fly . . . even if he panicked, with that same, uncontrollable panic so familiar to all the guys up there), as his own strength swept through him, talons sunk deep into flesh, he would have liked to flatten himself against the earth and eat, drink . . . oh, to unlace, to expose, to squeeze, to crush!

Stunned by this landscape that made him feel satisfied and terrified in turn, encumbered by his crutches, James set off again.

He felt tired. Nights had become a curse. Either he woke

The Colour of Distance

and, half asleep, couldn't tell any more whether he was really suffering, if time had passed or if he was still a dependent child, living in a mysterious world, not terrified by death and silence. Or he had nightmares and as soon as he fell asleep again he was plunged back down into the same dream about a pack of kids at his heels. He never leapt out of bed in the mornings any more, to slip into the bathroom and emerge as fresh as a daisy to look for his wife, calling her his butterfly.

He remembered his mother, maybe because of this wild place that would have terrified her, so pale, so afraid of everything (oh Lord, how afraid she was every day knowing he was up there working on the rooftops). How good it had been to have that distant hand, when he was a child, screening his face from the sun whenever it popped out suddenly from behind the clouds.

'This is a fantastic place,' his wife said. 'It's a good thing we came, it would've been silly of us not to take advantage of the special deal that's cost us practically nothing . . . even if it's actually pretty touristy. Did you see how many buses were here when we arrived? It's unbelievable how many people come on these trips. We'd never have known a thing about it if . . . I mean if . . . Oh, you used to work so much, we never went on any trips, did we?'

'Please . . .' he murmured.

'What a clanger, I've really put my foot in it!' she said, her soft hand stroking his cheek. 'I'm really sorry, James, but you have to admit that now I've got you all to myself I'm hardly going to complain about it . . . not very likely, is it?'

She shrugged one shoulder, just one, and as if there was nothing wrong, moved off round the walkway again, in front of him, between the overhanging rocks, carrying their things in a backpack, her bright curls topping her silhouette, bouncing on her shoulders in time with the rhythm of her quick steps.

Yes, her whole being, she was light, and he was surprised to find he was irritated for the first time by this lightness that he'd considered a blessing for so long.

Just then, James heard a noise from the long grass he was walking past, a rustling, a crackling, a murmur.

'Here chicky chicky!'

Intrigued, the young man stepped to the side of the path, towards the bushes. There, kneeling on the ground and leaning forward, a stick in her hand, with her hat thrown aside and her long ringlets spreading round her shoulders, the little girl in the white dress who wasn't interested in infinity or the passing of time, was poking at something.

James swung himself closer on his crutches, and saw, lying under a bush, a dead bird, grey, its eyes painfully closed, its wings spread wide and half buried in the sand as if it had wanted to embrace this world before departing it, a dead bird, a little soul, that the little girl was pushing at with her stick.

'Come on, come on, get up,' she was saying. 'Get up.'

'It looks to me as though it can't get up any more,' the young man cut in.

Neither surprised nor frightened, the little girl turned: her small face was covered in freckles and framed in curls. Her eyes were huge. She was very pretty. A power radiated from her. She looked at James as if he were her teacher and she had to stand up to him because she'd understood that half the time, without meaning any harm by it, grown-ups talked nonsense.

'Yes it can,' she said obstinately.

And then James felt his wife's hand slip beneath his arm.

'Are you coming?' she asked.

Translated from the French by Jean Anderson

Pierre Furlan

Pierre Furlan was the third French Writer in Residence at the Randell Cottage in Wellington where he spent a few happy months between October 2004 and March 2005. He has now returned to his home in Paris. He is the author of three novels, a play, a collection of stories called *L'Atelier de Barbe-Bleue* ('Bluebeard's Workshop', 2002) and a number of essays on contemporary writers. He is also a noted translator and has helped make New Zealand literature better known in France by translating Elizabeth Knox, Alan Duff and Geoff Cush. 'Paekakariki' was written during his residency in Wellington.

Paekakariki

You would tell me: 'It's time.'
Then you'd go away and I'd get up.

The strange thing is that your words come back to me today, lying here on the beach, my left ear filled with the low sighing of the waves collapsing on the sand and my right buzzing with the cicadas' shrill chorus. Maybe it's this racket that allows your words to surface.

Steven and the others didn't want to stay out in the sun, so they'd gone for a walk along the water's edge, past the driftwood on the high tide line, between the twisted grey dead branches swept out to sea by the rivers, carried on the tides, finally abandoned here. Couldn't we use them to build a big fire and roast a sheep? We would dedicate the fat and the smoke to the Gods, according to custom, and when the juice ran down our fingers we'd wipe them on the sand or on our bodies.

You wouldn't approve. You'd just shake your head and I'd know.

What I remember most is the sound of your voice; of your face I can recall only a certain sadness, and perhaps a trace of something morbid. There was a snideness, a subtle poison, in people's compliments when they said you looked like Humphrey Bogart.

When I open my eyes again I notice that something's different: the colours have started to bleed. I see it first in the sky where the blue has torn itself away from the white, trailing streaks across the outlines, then in the leaves with their green smudged over the edges like a careless painting, and even further away on the flag where the orange and yellow have drifted outside the margins. I tell myself all this must be because of the glare, I try blinking, but nothing goes back into its proper place. That's the sort of day it is, I've known times when even words couldn't come close to what they were supposed to mean, when I took comfort in the thought that at least my shadow was hard on my heels. And through all these gaps there's a white, unreal light spreading across the sand and the water. It shines down on a bird just in front of me, a black one, not much bigger than a blackbird or a tui. He's full of confidence, attacking a piece of rotten wood with his beak. As the splinters fly he pulls out worms or insects and swallows them, lifting his head towards the sky, then starting to peck again. A fearless bird that doesn't even let the gulls put him off when they try to settle right beside him with a great flapping of wings.

Hammer away, I tell him, hammer away! As if he was avenging some old grievance of mine. His beak is so strong, so precise: Katherine Mansfield's pen must have been just like that. He gives me so much pleasure, to me he's a perfect machine, one of my dreams come to life. Every rap of his beak announces it proudly: summer has come to Paekakariki, and all our sins are forgiven!

And yet I'm the one who frightened this wonderful bird away, sitting up because there was a long line, a whole army of children approaching from the far end of the beach. They looked like bees in their brown and orange striped shirts, with their hats sitting roundly on their heads. They stamped their little feet on the hard sand and held their arms close in to their chests like folded wings, buzzing as they came, 'Fit, fit, fittest.' They went past very close, not looking at me, in a long procession back to the slowpokes, the very last ones, the lost

The Colour of Distance

ones. The out-of-breath little girl who sighed through a bubble of spit: 'We're training . . . we're getting fit.'

After they'd gone I felt lonely and decided to go to the café to look for the people who'd brought me here in their car. The colours still weren't properly inside their outlines, but I wasn't going to let it bother me any more, no, I was going to pretend today was just one more of those ordinary days whose only merit is that they eventually end.

In the café we hid it all away behind laughter and jokes, and I remember feeling a bit envious of the green parrot painted on the wall because it could just sit there without having to say a thing.

We were drinking wine in spite of the heat. By the third glass, the bubbles had started to sing and Tony suggested that the shops and cafés in the street should be knocked flat, including the wall with the painted green parrot, and rebuilt further down beside the sea. Put a bulldozer through the lot and start again from scratch. It would be good for business, he said, and we'd be sitting there looking at the wide blue horizon. We'd see ourselves as if in a mirror, and the surf would sing softly in our hearts . . .

Steven didn't agree, absolutely not; he thought that was the kind of idea some Nazi architect might've had.

Katie had been studying the room for some time. 'I can prove I'm a lesbian,' she said.

Everyone thought everyone else was a riot.

The shadows were lengthening like knives and we shouldn't have stayed in our bare feet. Lizzie told us the few acres of land the Wakefield Company allocated to one of her ancestors were so steep that a horse couldn't stay upright on the slope. She looked at the railway line. 'No trains in those days either.' Her ancestor, she went on, had given everything he had to buy this land that he thought was flat—he'd even gone into debt—only to find himself faced with such a sharp incline he had to climb it on hands and knees, like a goat.

'He didn't commit suicide?' I asked.

'I'm here, aren't I?' she answered.

As if that proved anything. I'm here too. But her reply had silenced me. The wine in my glass started to swirl, and I told myself that you were there as well. This was the second time today I'd felt your presence, and I still didn't understand why. Usually you were far away, or rather you were so deeply ingrained in me that you'd taken the form of some of my thoughts and gestures, and this made you invisible. But there you were, that afternoon in Paekakariki, probably because of the gap between the colours and the outlines. My soul, when you died, was still a child's—is it ever any different for us, in our father's eyes? The thought that you might be inside my soul filled me with speechless horror; up till now I'd always fought to be alone in my body. Had I lost that fight too?

The only time we'd clashed that I could remember, you'd won hands down by showing me how inhuman my strength was. One Sunday morning on the freeway, on the way home from church, you were talking to me as you drove along about your difficult life, about Mom and the divorce, and I rebelled, I said I wasn't the one you should be pouring your heart out to. The car swerved across into another lane, just crumpled metal and nobody died that time, but it was like a dress rehearsal. Standing there on the hard shoulder you looked a bit distraught, and there I was, stiff as a board on the outside and totally shocked on the inside, wondering how mere words could have had such an impact. My words.

You were the child, and, at fourteen, I was the father trying to stop you from destroying us.

Now I realised that I'd started feeling sick when Lizzie made that comment about being here. Because in fact I haven't been entirely here for a long time. I believe I've forgotten you, I know I wouldn't be able to describe you, and yet just hearing you breathing on the other end of the phone would be enough for me to know it's you. Or else you turn up in one of my dreams. I'm driving and you're sitting in the back seat wearing your flying jacket. You don't say much— your worried expression is enough to tell me I'm not going in the right direction. Should I make a right turn, or go left? Turn round and go back? I stare into the rearview mirror, I study the expression in your eyes and try to read there the way ahead. I don't have an accident.

I can't drive all by myself, but my shrink insists that you

obviously committed suicide all by yourself. Nothing to do with me or what I said. Nobody could have stopped you, he says.

If only you could really leave me, die properly. That wouldn't be the end of me, would it?

'I'm here, aren't I?' Lizzie repeats with a strange pride, as if my question had offended her.

We're the survivors, and therefore the fittest. The product of hundreds of thousands of years of evolution, that's us. Could there be any greater proof of our worth?

I feel as if we're rising with the wind. In the street some Jesus freak has set up a sign. He calls out 'Jesus loves you', pointing to this love bleeding on a dried out old wooden cross. His offsider tries to hand us pamphlets, printed in big letters: NO, MAN IS NOT DESCENDED FROM THE APES. Isn't it strange, this insistence on believing that God wanted him, specially, to be just the way he is? Perhaps his God even speaks to him, as well. Are they born-agains? Steven asks. Are they the ones who believe in the rapture and in Armageddon? They're all going to Heaven in ten years' time, or three. I wish it was straight away, this evening, we're so keen to see them go flying up.

I say 'we', and I feel sad because I know you wouldn't want to see me in such company.

A quarter of an hour in the car and we wind up at Lizzie's place. She wants to show us the two deer that live behind her house, in a pen where they haven't eaten all the bushes yet. One of the deer is small, light brown, and looks like Bambi; the other is big and dark and lifts his antlered head, anxious. You can see his muscles twitching under his black coat; he makes you want to touch him because you can tell he's poised for flight, and when you touch him you'll have that delicious feeling of taming something wild. Lizzie passes us some bok choy leaves: if you push them through the holes in the fence and wave them about the deer will come and eat out of your hands, she says.

But when Steven and Katie put their Chinese cabbage through the fence, it's Lizzie's dog that rushes up, a very pale cocker spaniel that's managed to slip into the enclosure: he stands on his hind legs and snatches one of the leaves and chews and swallows it. And Lizzie laughs her head off. The surprise she wanted to show us was her vegetarian cocker spaniel, Snowy. He got so jealous watching everyone making a fuss of the deer, she says, that he started eating what they eat. He's stealing their limelight, and when it comes down to it *they're all just children.* 'Isn't that right, Snowy?' she asks, stroking him as he rolls on his back at her feet. She goes on about the Garden of Eden where no animal ate another, where they must all have been vegetarians. But Katie protests: what makes us think plants don't suffer?

This dog makes me sick. He didn't degrade himself to this extent all on his own. He reminds me of those idiotic, saccharine versions of 'Little Red Riding Hood' where the wolf can't even eat the grandmother any more. Snowy, Lizzie's cocker spaniel, Lizzie's son. Suddenly I feel sorry for him, I hate Lizzie, and then I pull myself together, my disgust seems over the top—after all, even if she's flattered that her dog has turned into an occasional vegetarian, jealous of the deer, is she really responsible for this? This unnatural canine, this pseudo-human rolling on his back and eating cabbage, this poor castrated show-off, deprived of meat, sleeping at his mistress's feet or on her bed, maybe even *in* her bed, he's like me, after all. I'd already felt a connection with that black bird early this afternoon. Only human beings seem eternally distant from me. And I wondered if that's because of you. If I could blame you for it.

We set off again. I found myself in a car with people whose names I didn't know, and had that rather pleasant feeling of being nowhere, always between two places, when we pulled up at the house of the artist with blue hair. Actually she'd woven lengths of neon blue wool into her dyed black hair, and her house, huge and glowing in the light of the setting sun, stood in the middle of an artificial-looking garden. Walking down the mosaic-decorated pathways edged with big blue flowers, passing the stone benches where statues covered in ceramic fragments were baking in the sun—they were couples, sometimes grotesque with their wings and crowns, but mostly, touchingly naïve—it was as if I was moving towards the edge of the world. Or rather it was in the big sitting room flooded with light, in front of the fireplace with its solid totara surround, between the imposing animal-shaped sculptures and the absurd machines that reminded me of Tinguely's, that I began to feel that the world was ending. The feeling came from the music playing very softly, apparently night and day, a neverending music with a rhythm as repetitive as the cicadas', the best-known tunes of last century in a monotonous arrangement, the original melodies so bland that although they were recognisable you could really only hear them from memory, and the world in turn was no more substantial than nostalgia. From this point on, everything would be smooth and muffled, as if buried under a very gentle snowfall that would deaden our voices and our footsteps.

That's when I heard you say it again.

It's time.

In the past, when you said these words you'd be standing behind my bedroom door, telling me it was time to get up and go to school. I could probably hear the resignation in your voice, because after you'd gone these words always struck me as being your way of preparing for death. Of letting yourself be weighed down, day after day.

But in the house of the blue-haired artist, what was this 'time'? Time to leave, time to stay? To follow you, or to go out into the world? Your time, mine? Were we still tied together by these words, like a piece of rope with each of us holding on to one end? I stood there for a moment, perplexed, lost amongst all these objects that had no proper name any more, and then my own voice, unexpectedly, very clear:

'I don't know you.'

Translated from the French by Jean Anderson

Pierre Furlan   121

Geoff Cush

Geoff Cush (born 1956) is a Wellington-based writer. *Son of France* was translated into French by Pierre Furlan. Set in the author's imagined 'beautiful French colony of New Zealand' in 1930, the novel is a funny, cleverly-realised conceit. This is the second chapter.

from **Son of France**

The Shattered Calm of the Bay

Lieutenant Verdier lunched alone under a blue-and-white striped awning at a little restaurant beside the fishing harbour at Akaroa. He ate a large dish of oysters à la Polonaise harvested from natural beds a few kilometres down the coast, then sat back, smoking and watching the men working on the boats.

I should leave now, he thought. He was anticipating the aphrodisiac effect of the oysters. But the sea breeze on his face was good enough for the moment, and the moment was an important part of his philosophy. He was always reminding himself: I will never be here again.

The Maori waitress came out onto the terrace and collected his plate. He smiled at her.

'Those oysters.' He raised his right hand and kissed the joined tips of thumb and first finger. 'Perfection!'

'Glad you enjoyed them, Lieutenant.' She said it with an emphasis that made him look at her to see if she was being insolent. Earlier she had brought a glass for red wine with his half-bottle of Chablis. He had corrected her with a clear conscience—his dissatisfaction was the force that civilised the world. But her manner had suggested that she could hardly see what the fuss was about and that it was too hot to make her go back and forth to change one glass. Now, he decided, she has had time to realise that I was right. She is pleased that I am satisfied. She has learned something about the serving of wines. He tipped her generously, then he put on his kepi but did not move from his seat.

122

Juliette is waiting, he thought. The later I leave, the faster I'll go.

He cast an affectionate eye over his motorcycle, a 1928 Terrot 500, gleaming in the sunlight just beyond the terrace rail. The Terrot was his true love. His vast pleasure in it was only slightly diminished by the fact that it was powered by an English engine. 'Zere are some sings zey do better zan us,' he said aloud. He was practising his English but could never get away from that ludicrous, humiliating, zed.

He walked along the quay, past the boats and the brown men bringing the catches ashore. The happiest aspect of the meeting of French and Maori was a shared love of the fruits of the sea.

The street became a track that went up the hill. He took his time climbing up towards the old mission church. The sun was on the water below him, on the back of his neck and on the white sand of the beach where the first settlers had landed. It seared and flaked the paint on the iron roofs of the first houses, now rusting corrugated unlikely monuments of national heritage.

Later the bourgeoisie had come out, bringing their accomplishments and cash, when they were sure that the English had really gone. But at first it was just peasants and tradesmen and sundry other gulls of the Nanto-Bordelaise company with no idea why they were there or what would happen next, a meagre force augmented by a few red-capped sailors who were sick of the sea and soon got sicker of that strip of land between the bay and the bush. Every Frenchman visiting Akaroa was expected to commemorate them solemnly at the church they had built on the hill. Any Frenchman was pleased to do so.

To the breathless walker at the top of the hill the bay posed questions. How can I have this view and be inside it? How can I drink all the water and still swim in it? Dilemmas of modern life. A breeze came up, ruffling the water and billowing his shirt. The view was in any case too full of light. He did not believe in the settlers' god but it would be good to rest his eyes in the dark spaces of their hammer-beam kauri roof.

Then he saw, way below, five or six kids, Maori and

Pakeha, running along the beach road towards the fishing harbour. They were running with the unmistakable intent of young humans on the scent of fun. It was as though they had just heard a circus was in town. He thought of calling out: 'Stop where you are!' But that was no good. From this distance nothing would be any good short of shooting them. Appealing though the idea was, French officers did not carry guns. He started back down the hill, running, his boots raising dust on the track.

When he came in sight of the restaurant a circle of small brown and white faces turned in his direction. Between their arms and legs he could see the shining metal tubing. The machine was still upright, at least. He calculated how long it had taken him to get down the hill, how much time they had had for fiddling, scratching and unscrewing. Then he saw the waitress standing at the door of the restaurant.

'It's okay, Lieutenant,' she said. 'I've got my eye on them.'

Her folded arms laid a spell of respectfulness over the little raiding-party.

'Thank you.' He thanked a god he did not believe in that he had tipped her well. The kids parted to let him through, not without a certain resentful shuffling. The fact that they had got there first made the machine, in some sense, theirs. He put on his goggles. Seven pairs of eyes watched him sceptically. The waitress in her doorway asked, 'What's it like riding one of them?'

'Almost as good as your oysters.'

She laughed. 'Better than that, I reckon.'

He climbed onto the seat and smiled at her. She was longing to go with him.

'See ya later, Lieutenant.'

'Probably not,' he answered accurately, then remembered it was just a figure of speech, a local idiom. 'Yeah, see you later.'

He opened the fuel line and set the ignition lever. The kids stood silently around the motorcycle, evidently doubtful about his ability to work it.

'Watch out for the stones, kids. Kia tupato i nga pohatu, tamariki.'

They backed away a few centimetres, but his first kick was

weak. The machine still dozed in the sun, the little sceptics raised their hands to their mouths and tittered. A second kick and it came to life. Verdier grinned, working the throttle, making the engine backfire. The noise crashed around the houses and hills. The kids shrieked and danced. The birds along the wharf betook themselves out to sea. With a last wave at the waitress he put the machine in gear and blasted off, leaving her to patch up the damaged faces.

He came up the port hill, crouching to cheat the wind, with this new thing in the world, the twist throttle, under his hand. Farmers on foot and bicycle and horseback stopped and turned. 'There goes France!' they said. Their sluggish lives froze in salute as he flashed past at seventy kilometres an hour. His slipstream was a tricolour.

Above eighty-five, he did not think of speed as French or having any meaning at all. He was no longer an apostle of the civilising mission. His mind was sucked clean by the rushing air, by moment and momentum. He was out to beat his personal best, to reach the top of the first hill in fifteen minutes.

He was looking down at the white spokes of Sainte-Chapelle radiating across the Normandy Plain. His heart was filled with pride. He was French again. Riding a motorcycle to visit another man's wife was absolutely French.

The aerial view of the city brought Lyautey's dictum to mind: A town should be set in a country as a picture is set on a wall. The great man had said it about Morocco, but surely in the bustling hub of the Normandy Plain it had been most brilliantly realised. Verdier had seen the desert but not its romance, only scarcity and competition. He remembered the staring sheep in the fields of rocks. Here on the Plain, after four months of summer, the woolly blobs still had their heads down in the grass. If I had to be a sheep, he thought, weaving down the bends, looking across to the ranges where the alpine rivers rose, I would prefer to live here. Instead I am a man on a motorcycle, and this is the place for me too.

He leaned hard on the tight bends, then relaxed through the gentler curves and on the straight he opened it out and went with the wind.

Damien Wilkins

Born in Lower Hutt in 1963, Damien Wilkins is the author of four novels, a collection of stories and another of poems. His first novel, *The Miserables*, which won the New Zealand Book Award for Fiction in 1994 and was published internationally, is a subversive commentary (at several removes) on Victor Hugo's *Les Misérables*.

from The Miserables

When Healey's brother was approaching high-school age, a period known as the French Terror was launched. Now the grandfather, restless with being a pupil of his French ladies—the women who ran the French Club to which he'd belonged for more than fifteen years following his retirement—sought his own students. Once a fortnight he would come to his daughter's house with his small blackboard, which he propped against the dining-room table, and his chalk, and he would proceed to write up those phrases and sentences that were to be said over and over again until the mouths of the children might arrive naturally at the shapes of this, the finest language. The vowels, he said, once the vowels are in place. *'Rose originale.' 'C'est difficile.'*

In addition to the dining-room lessons, there was the morning phone call. Each weekday at eight o'clock it was understood that Healey's sister would answer the phone by saying in a loud voice, because the grandfather was by now quite deaf: *'Oui?'* She would then respond to questioning with the three or four phrases her grandfather had previously supplied. *'Maman est dans la maison,'* she would shout into the receiver several times before the vowels had properly assembled, each time pulling a longer face and miming a strangulation scene for her brothers waiting their turn. The phone would then be handed to Healey's brother and the same phrases would ring out, so that by the time Healey was up, he knew by heart the correct sounds to make though he scarcely understood a word he was saying.

On his eleventh birthday, his grandfather gave Healey a book by the French author he said was his personal favorite, Victor Hugo. It was a heavy book, hardcover, brown with an elegant border of intricate gold curls whose design Healey liked to trace with a finger. His eyes closed. Inside, the pages were made of more than a thousand sheets of the finest tissue paper, though Healey could only verify this several days after receiving the book. When his grandfather presented him with the package and he first opened the book, Healey had been unable to tell anything about it, so anxious and muddled had he been on seeing that the title of this favorite French author's work embossed in gold lettering on the spine was in the language whose vowels he could place but whose sense he believed he would never fathom: *Les Misérables*. The Miserables, he said to himself, the Miserables, he repeated again and again, searching for an adequate translation. Now, he thought, he would be uncovered for the fake he was. Of course, the book was in English, only its title had remained as the author had written it, but Healey, on first looking at the words in the grip of this French-panic, failed to recognise any of them. It was all he could do to close the book and admire the gold design against the brown while his grandfather, luckily, began to rehearse those details of Victor Hugo's life that had led him to hold that artist in the highest regard—his unstable childhood; his political idealism; his gloriously productive exile; the death of his sons; the insanity of his daughter; the treachery of his friend Saint-Beuve in stealing his wife; the epic obstacles overcome along the way, until there was now a street in every French town bearing that great name.

Alan Knowles

Alan Knowles is a Wellington photographer who has exhibited and published widely. Among his recent projects is a series of images relating to outdoor sports (a selection of which were published in *Sport 22* in 1999). Other subjects he has explored are creative dance in primary schools, scenes from a biscuit factory and images of tramping and hunting in the New Zealand wilderness. He has also taken photographs of New Zealand writers, many of which are included in the 2005 National Library Gallery exhibition 'Main Trunk Lines: New Zealand Poetry'. In 2002 he was commissioned by the French Embassy, Wellington, to take portrait photographs of the visiting French writers at the Randell Cottage.

French Writers in the Randell Cottage

The Randell Cottage is located in Thorndon, Wellington, a short distance from the Katherine Mansfield Birthplace, and was gifted by the Price family as a writers' residence. The Randell Cottage Creative New Zealand Writers Residency provides accommodation and financial support for one French writer per year, and is administered by the Randell Cottage Writers Trust in partnership with the Embassy of France and the New Zealand–France Friendship Fund and with Creative New Zealand

The first three holders of the Residency were:

Nadine Ribault, 2002–3

Charles Juliet (photographed with M. L.), 2003–4

Pierre Furlan, 2004–5

Charles Juliet

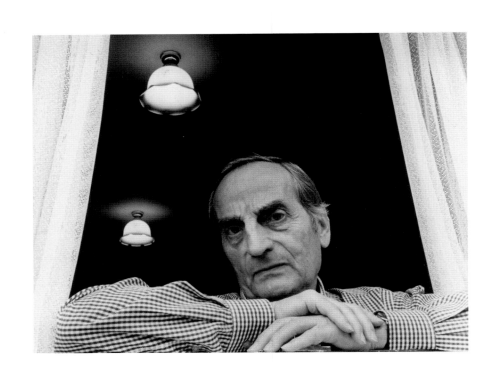

Pierre Furlan

Nadine Ribault

Nadine Ribault

Visiting Janet Frame

I won't forget visiting Janet Frame. I'd been told over and over again that it wasn't possible to meet her, that she kept to herself, that she was 'uncontactable', that she was hiding out in the South Island, in Dunedin, and from the start this struck me as strange—not that someone could live like that, choose to do so, yes that can happen, and does happen—but that this story was so universally believed made me suspicious.

'She doesn't see anyone any more. She lives on her own. Shut away. Every human being has a protective shell, you know, but not her. So she keeps to herself. The door is closed. You won't be able to meet her. No one meets her.'

Looking back, I think essentially that I simply refused to believe it.

Her novels—the unforgettable *State of Siege*, for example— her autobiography, her poetry, all hinted to me that it was impossible for this to be true. And then there were the photos of her that everyone has seen. I could picture her face, her expression, that little half-smile. There was the major biography that had been published. The articles. There were the small, barely visible signs and her sense of humour—she had a wonderful sense of humour—which told me that the absolute withdrawal from society, the notorious standoffishness, the unbreachable distance were, like any rumour, not to be taken at face value.

So I wrote to her. I sent her copies of my books. I told her I was a writer in residence in New Zealand—a new residency set up in Wellington to mirror the Katherine Mansfield award which had taken Janet Frame herself to my own country, to Menton and the Villa Isola Bella where Katherine Mansfield had spent a few months, some of them happy, but most of them under the terrible shadow of the ravages of tuberculosis, which would carry her off at the age of 34.

129

I wrote to Janet Frame to say that I would be in Dunedin on my way to visit Fiordland.

I think I wrote some other things as well.

Then I was away from Wellington for a while. Fortunately this meant I couldn't spend all my time loitering beside my letterbox. When I got back from Auckland ten days later the box was full, but no letter from Janet Frame. Five minutes later, there was her voice, sounding hesitant and embarrassed, on the answering machine . . .

'Venez me voir.' Come and see me.

In Dunedin, on Friday the 29th of October 2002, I took a taxi to go to her home in St Kilda. I had the driver drop me at the end of Oxford Street because for some unknown reason—to get used to the idea, to calm my racing thoughts, to get my shyness under control—I wanted to walk up the street. I thought about the suffering Janet Frame had endured, the trials she'd been through, about how she'd survived.

I'm normally full of apprehension, but on that day I didn't for one second—which is strange—doubt that she would be there. And yet just the previous day I'd been warned to expect this and not be too disappointed by it, because she generally didn't keep the appointments she made.

People can't have read Janet Frame, I thought as I walked along this street with its little lookalike bungalows, each with its tiny garden and handful of flowers, if they misunderstand her this way.

But in any case this wasn't very important. What was important was the short time we would spend together; I wanted to enjoy it and make the most of what was for me a special, happy occasion.

When I got to her house I went up the two or three steps towards it then stopped, hesitating, because the only entrance I could see was a little gateway and a path leading to the garden. I didn't know what to do. On my left there were French windows shrouded in thick greyish curtains. No flowers. No movement. No sound. No sign of life. No door. Nothing. Later, thinking back, I suspected that someone may have been watching me from inside the house, but I'm far from certain of this . . .

The Colour of Distance

I shivered briefly as the statements and predictions of the various people who had warned me went through my mind. I raised my hand, waving away this clutter of negative thoughts, and knocked on one of the panes of the French window.

There was a rustling behind me, then . . .

'Are you Nadine?'

. . .Janet Frame indicated I should go through the gateway and along the side of the house to where the door was. I was too shy to go past her. She held out her hand in invitation. I misunderstood her gesture and kissed her on the cheek in greeting. She blushed and smiled warmly at me.

Her eyes were striking, a light, bright blue. I did recognise her. I'd been worried that I wouldn't. She was both extraordinarily shy and attentive at the same time.

In the hallway I felt as though I were choking, from the musty smell of animals and cooking combined with my panicky feeling that I would never be able to focus on the reasons for my visit.

Why had I come here to disturb her? I thought suddenly—a question which had never once crossed my mind when people told me that in fact she didn't like to be disturbed. In that split second I realised that perhaps I was going to waste her time, that I had nothing to give her in return for everything she would unquestionably be giving me. I didn't want to pry and I knew it was out of the question—since we didn't know one another at all—to talk about things which would be too personal or private.

Whatever would we talk about?

'My cat is sixteen years old.'

She pointed out the cat, curled up in a ball beside the heater in the bedroom.

We went through the kitchen and into the room with the French windows and the thick greyish curtains: this was both her study and her sitting room. She sat down, then got up again to phone her sister who of course would be joining us, along with her husband.

I don't know which of us was the more embarrassed.

Silence fell.

Our expected visitors arrived.

Nadine Ribault   131

Janet Frame introduced her brother-in-law and her sister and all four of us drove to Dunedin's Botanical Gardens where we looked at the roses, *multiflora, rugosa, luciae, x damascena, muscosa,* and had something to eat in the coffee-shop.

Janet Frame talked to me about Albert Camus and Marguerite Duras; she had read and loved their work.

'Especially *L'Exil et le royaume.*'

And Virginia Woolf.

Her sister talked about England and Trafalgar Square.

We commented on the swans we could see through the windows, moving about on the water below.

Gradually Janet Frame's silences became longer and longer. Her sister carried on talking. And her brother-in-law and I tried to communicate despite the noise level in the coffee-shop and his wife's conversation; I think half the time my answers to his well-meaning questions were completely off-topic.

Suddenly he stood up and took out his camera.

'You don't mind?' Janet Frame asked me.

I said no, I didn't mind (sensing an appeal in her question).

'And you?'

'I hate it,' she whispered, leaning towards me, 'but he always does it.'

She was making an ally of me.

Outside we were back amongst the *multiflora, rugosa, luciae, x damascena, muscosa* roses. I wanted to be alone with her.

'I would like to have a talk with you.'

I didn't know exactly what I wanted to talk to her about, but I did want to talk to her. I was suddenly aware of time slipping away from me. She answered, as if she were speaking to a child who is tired of the outing and has had enough of the *multiflora, rugosa, luciae, x damascena, muscosa* roses . . .

'Let's go home.'

Walking with her cane, she quite unexpectedly took my arm.

Back in the car, she asked her brother-in-law if he would mind going back via the beach at St Clair, where we got out of the car again and Janet Frame walked off, away from us.

The Colour of Distance

Suddenly her sister's husband wanted to take some more photos. He got out his camera which I noticed he'd kept in his pocket. He took photos of us, his wife and me, saying they would be fantastic because there in the background was Janet walking back towards us.

The wind was cold and the waves were breaking icily on the beach.

Janet Frame gestured towards the horizon.

'There's nothing between Dunedin and the Antarctic. I need to come here in the winter to feel this icy wind. That's why I live in Dunedin.'

I wanted to answer, to say, I know what you mean, I live by the sea because I need to walk along the beach to breathe in that freshness.

We got back into the car. On the way, she pointed out the footpaths, the parking areas . . .

'There are so many cars and so few people in town these days.'

I think she meant 'real people', people who don't huddle inside iron carcasses, brooding and depressed, crushed by fear and separation.

Finally we were back in her study, behind the thick greyish curtains. She picked up my book of short stories and in her moving voice read out the first page or so. Looking up, I noticed that her desk, on our left, was tidied up as if she were going away, the computer covered with a cloth, the typewriter with another cloth, practically nothing lying about, no books, just a little pile of paper, some pencils perhaps—I don't remember very clearly. I do remember that I found this strange. I know it's very time-consuming to tidy your desk, it's an act of little value that you don't even bother to do most of the time, letting things pile up (like in her kitchen, where there was such a mess that her cat wouldn't have been able to find her kittens, assuming she had any). What a contrast between the study and the rest of the house!

Here, everything was tidy.

In Wellington, Dunedin, Auckland, lots of people said she wasn't writing any more.

She told me she was writing. Spontaneously, because

I hadn't dared to ask any of the questions in the back of my mind. Docile, I let her lead the conversation, and the silences.

She broke off and suggested we go into the garden. We went outside. It wasn't a big garden but she guided me along. She asked me if I'd like to go into the shed. My eyes must have practically popped out of my head and I may even have answered, no thank you. Worried, I wondered if perhaps she'd got the wrong idea, thinking I wanted to satisfy my curiosity, as others before me had done perhaps, by poking my nose into every corner of her house and garden and even this old shed where she probably kept her garden tools or stored old bits and pieces away from the dust.

She smiled and we went back inside the house.

The sun was shining faintly on the desk, highlighting a few books and assorted objects. News spreads like wildfire in this country; a well-informed teacher had mentioned to me the day before that since I was going to meet her I'd probably be astonished to see that she had hardly any books. Was this man right, was I wrong? I'd refused to believe him—it's not possible for a writer not to have books, I'd said.

The atmosphere was welcoming and peaceful and the décor utterly simple. Janet Frame refused to possess things. She rented houses. She moved often.

She talked about the biography which had been published.

'Your life's like a play, you have to accept that you can't control it, you have to accept the director's interpretation.'

Then she fell silent.

She always left silences after she spoke.

Later, we talked about Europe, about her travels, about Ibiza. I was witnessing a miracle: she was dipping into her past, bringing up handfuls of pearls. She was laughing, animated, bubbling with happiness. But still so few words.

'Of all my books, *Intensive Care* is the one I'm most attached to. You really don't want to see the books?'

'Books?' I said, startled.

'In the shed.'

We went back out of the house, one behind the other—

anyone watching us would have thought we were going on and off stage, in a play—back out to the shed where, not half an hour earlier, I'd said I didn't want to go in, that no, I wasn't curious.

She unlocked the door with a tiny key and inside, to my absolute delight, I discovered dozens and dozens of books on shelves lining all four walls of the shed, in cardboard boxes, or piled on the floor or on a table, on old chairs, everywhere.

Janet Frame propped her cane in a corner and knelt down to pull out the bottom layer of books. There she was, surrounded by books, laughing.

'Now what's this? and this?'

Piled together, all mixed up, were foreign and New Zealand novels, volumes of poetry, biographies, her own books and their French or Italian translations and their American editions.

'What language is this?'

She searched high and low while I watched, head on one side, then the other.

She found a book by Nadine Gordimer. She really admired her work and had met her once in the United States.

She found a book by Jane Austen.

'She had all she needed to write about in one village. You don't have to go to the Antarctic.'

She gave me *The Lagoon* and *You Are Now Entering the Human Heart*.

We went back into the house and she asked me what I was working on. I was having trouble at the time. For weeks I'd been feeling discouraged, incompetent, accusing myself of trying to do things that were beyond my reach. I couldn't get on with it. There were two wild beasts fighting within me, ferocious, vicious, and I just wanted one of them to win, the fight to be over.

She waved it away.

'All writers struggle to write. There are always times of distress.'

She looked down.

She wasn't sad or depressed, she said nothing desperate, but she was painfully cast down into her solitude and I sensed her tragic thoughts behind her silence.

Her simplicity was for me something unique and extraordinary.

And I was in such great need of something unique and extraordinary, that was surely what had brought me here to see her. Perhaps she had sensed this, I don't know, but I am certain that she was highly sensitive and knew that for many people a writer is little more than some creature onto whose back they load their rumours, piling them up into a burden which gets heavier year by year, unverified stories, further and further from the truth, rumours in total contradiction of the writer's work.

Suddenly she said . . .

'Keep on writing.'

Keep on writing. The sentence she must have said to herself, over and over, through the difficult times. It's what the London doctor told her, years before, saving her from the worst, from being shut up for life on her return to New Zealand (after an eight-year period already spent in and out of psychiatric institutions where she had undergone innumerable electric shock treatments, which she told me had damaged her memory), and from an imminent lobotomy. This London doctor who with one stroke of his pen deleted the fateful diagnosis of schizophrenia made by her New Zealand doctors.

Keep on writing.

Hold fast to the helm and don't let go.

Cling to the lifeline.

Whatever the obstacles.

Survive them all.

Even the abyss.

Then she talked to me about death.

'When you've gone,' she said as I was getting ready, 'I'll go for a little walk.'

It was hard for me to leave her.

Six months later she publicly acknowledged the truth of a rumour which had been circulating: her leukemia had worsened.

On the 29th of January 2004, dear Janet Frame, after a

difficult life in which writing was essentially the only source of light (I believe I'm right in saying that there was really no room for anything else in your life), you have gone to be part of that icy wind you spoke of. You have gone towards what you wouldn't allow yourself to explore—the invisible mystery of existence. This is what I choose to remember: on the day you allowed me to visit you, you smiled repeatedly (joyful smiles, your expression lit up with pleasure), assuring me that whatever our dramas and torments, life is still the most fascinating subject for us to explore.

Côte d'Opale, France
February 2004

Translated from the French by Jean Anderson

Charles Juliet

Born in the village of Jujurieux, Ain, in 1934, Charles Juliet has produced over 30 books of poetry, art criticism and autobiography. He has written with great passion on topics as diverse as Samuel Beckett and rugby football. Early in 2005, his *Au pays du long nuage blanc: Journal, Wellington août 2003–janvier 2004*, chronicling his time as second French Writer in Residence at the Randell Cottage, was published in France by POL. While in New Zealand he also wrote poems, three of which appeared in the *New Zealand Journal of French Studies* (November 2004), and *Trois poèmes par Charles Juliet*, with translations by Gregory O'Brien and Jessie Munro, was published in a handprinted edition by Brendan O'Brien at the Fernbank Studio, Wellington, 2004.

from Au pays du long nuage blanc

August 25th 2003—Wellington

Before, at the beginning of each day, I made up a timetable in my head and then I followed this timetable closely. But if in the course of the day I had to alter my plans, for example if I had to forgo some little treat, some small pleasure which I'd expected to use as a prop to get me through the hours, I was secretly upset. This need to organise things in advance was probably rooted in a certain anxiety. Now I no longer have to decide at the start of the day what it will be like. I let it develop as circumstances dictate. I value not being driven, and being flexible enough each time to accept willingly whatever comes along.

August 26th

Why am I writing these notes? I don't really know. I have no illusions as to their interest. But I must content myself with the insignificant little events which fill our days. I want to keep track of these little events. In the hope that they may add up to something meaningful and interesting which will give value to each one of them individually.

138

September 6th

In the Belgian restaurant we had to put up for an hour with the racket made by two couples seated at the next table: they'd turned a little girl of about two into a sideshow. Tickling her, encouraging her to show off, they kept laughing uproariously and making loud comments about what she was saying or doing. It was truly distressing. They were laughing and I was completely dismayed by the child being turned into some kind of puppet show.

September 7th

We'd been told this, and every day, in every situation it's confirmed: New Zealanders are very friendly people. They don't have that reserve we French are in the habit of hiding behind. They're relaxed, open, welcoming, only too happy to strike up a conversation with us.

September 12th

The woman M. L. met this afternoon told her about her five sisters. One day, one of them went to Chile. What she saw there—abject poverty, children who are given no education and have no future—was a revelation to her and changed her life. She decided to stay and to take action. She started to teach them. Then she founded a school. And now she's committed to developing what she has created. She has even taken Chilean nationality and will come back to New Zealand only occasionally, to see her family.

September 28th

Three days ago I met Chris Laidlaw, former All Black captain, a very talented player still remembered by rugby enthusiasts. He lived in Paris and Lyons for two years, studying and playing for the L.O.U. He knows France very well and is still on friendly terms with several French rugby players. We talked for only an hour, but we will meet up again.

He told me that in the last test match they played in England, the English realised from some of the New Zealanders' behaviour that they were different from the English. It was the first time such a thing had happened,

Charles Juliet

and the New Zealanders were very pleased about it. They'd been given proof that they existed in their own right, and not in relation to the inhabitants of the old country—also Her Majesty's subjects.

New Zealanders, I was told, have an identity problem. Their country is a young one, only recently established. In addition, they suffer from their isolation, their distance from Europe, from the countries of their ancestors—Scotland, Ireland, England. Sometimes, on some maps, their country is missing, and that's not at all appreciated. Not showing their islands is in some way to deny their existence.

The suicide rate is high amongst young people. I don't know whether the causes are the same as in other Western societies or whether there are specific causes.

One fact of considerable importance should also be noted: last winter when the Americans invaded Iraq, Great Britain went along with them. On this occasion, for the first time in its history, the government of New Zealand, which has a woman Prime Minister, didn't copy the position of the former Home country and decided that New Zealand troops would not take part in this unfortunate venture. This act of independence created a great stir throughout the country. What's more, France and New Zealand adopted the same position vis-à-vis this conflict, which helped to restore the friendship between our two countries, a friendship which had been severely damaged by the breathtakingly stupid *Rainbow Warrior* episode.

September 30th

It was one in the afternoon. Gradually it became very dark and the storm broke. On the thirteenth floor of this glass-walled building, we were inside a cloud, pushed over us and the city by the fierce gusts of a howling gale. Rain bucketed down. Curtains of it blew in, in horizontal waves, whipping violently against the windows. Water spouted, spurted, gushing down the building walls.

As I was standing near a window and the metal frame around it was out of sight, I was astonished for a moment to see that I was protected from the squalling rain although there was nothing visible between it and me.

There were several of us in this huge room, and I stayed to one side for a moment to concentrate on what was happening outside. The violence of Nature when she breaks loose and rages.

Yesterday, a meeting with students at Victoria University. The last question I was asked came from a woman, a teacher.

'You've written somewhere that you like cows. What have they taught you?'

It's a very long time since I last thought about the cows I used to herd when I was a boy, and obviously the question surprised me. But in a split second the answer came:

'Montaigne tells us to "move with the pace of things". Maybe the cows taught me to go at the same speed as they do, to move through life at the same deliberate pace.'

This answer came out before I'd had time to think about it. But now that I'm writing this note, I realise that what I said was just words. Words which say nothing at all about my relationship with those fine cud-chewing creatures. The boy I used to be was incapable of thinking, of learning anything from what humans, animals or things could have taught him. To the extent that he was a part of that world, he didn't see it, had no distance from it. He had to leave his village to begin to be aware of what filled his life at that time. No, I don't think the cows taught me anything, but they could have.

To make up for that over-hasty response, I would say on a more general level that I have never gone back on the values that were imprinted on me during my country childhood. These values were never explicitly stated. I absorbed them, you might say, with the air I breathed. Mama Ruffieux's example was the best possible teaching.

As we were leaving the university the teacher who'd asked me the last question offered to take us home in her car. But she took a detour on the way and drove us to the other side of the hill behind the cottage. She wanted to show us the entry points for the various walkways through the bush. Then she wanted to show us her house, which has a wonderful view over the harbour. When she left the house she'd forgotten to turn off the stew she was cooking. Since it wasn't burnt, she asked us to stay for dinner. Her husband arrived and we talked for a long time. But very often the flats and houses here aren't heated, which makes me even more convinced that Kiwis are rather special people. Since we were freezing, she took pity on us and decided to light the fire.

My birthday. A good opportunity to look at where I am at this stage in my life.

I can say that I am light, serene, that I am living a better life. Freed from my shackles, I stopped trying to imitate role models long ago, I feel free and independent. The fears, urges, tensions, shyness, those old wounds . . . , all of that has been transformed and has melded into a continuity which gives me a deeply appreciated sense of stability. And so I no longer have to struggle with those excessively violent emotions that used to trouble me, shattering my thoughts, making me incapable of facing up to what I needed to confront. I can see too that all the different categories of knowledge I've acquired over the years have finally settled into place, and I have the impression that my understanding of human beings and of life has really grown. My perceptions have refined themselves, my unbendingness has given way to flexibility, and as a result I am able to work more easily. All the same, what I have just written shouldn't lead anyone to conclude that there is no downside and that I am blissfully happy with what I am. I am still dissatisfied. I will therefore carry on ploughing my furrow, but I won't be concerned any more about what may or may not grow in the soil I have worked.

Two other things to note: although I have a good few years behind me, I'm not blasé. I still move through life with the same freshness, the same pleasure in accepting what it brings that I felt when I was young. Could this be in part the result of the naïvety people say I have? I don't know. What is certain is that I'm delighted not to be in the clutches of the disillusionment, the sullenness that takes hold of people whose lives are not moving forward.

I have to add too that my internal make-up is changing. I'm beginning to realise that I don't have too many more years ahead of me—always supposing that Fate grants them to me—and that I can no longer keep putting off until some undetermined time in the future the projects I have in mind. Sometimes I even think about death. But perhaps because I don't yet feel it as a real threat, it doesn't frighten me. I even try to contemplate it calmly. To prepare myself to greet it on the day.

October 12th

On a postcard which arrived several days ago, there's a photo, taken in the Cévennes, probably at the start of the 20th century. Women, a man, children, sitting in a semicircle, on their knees those big sacks they used for potatoes, and they are pulling silk cocoons off branches that have been cut from the mulberry trees. What really strikes me is the seriousness, the sadness of their expressions. I have often noticed in old photos how sad people of the working class were. Even taking into account the fact that being in front of a camera was stressful for them, it's still clear to me from their faces and the look in their eyes that they were deeply sad. That's not at all surprising either. People's lives were hard and pleasure was rare. People of my generation from working-class backgrounds very often also lived in difficult conditions when they were children. I remember . . . The snow, the endless winters, the unheated bedrooms with ice on the window panes, the damp sheets, the water I had to fetch from the fountain with my two cans in all weathers, the meagre meals, and the times when you had to squat down in the grass behind the cows, because you had to keep an eye on them all the time so nothing terrible would happen to them . . .

As I finish writing this, I think about African women walking miles with a jug on their heads and another in each hand, just to fetch water. Compared to those women and to what millions of people in underdeveloped countries live through, we were well-off. But when you're hungry it's no use telling yourself that others are worse off than you. And in any case we were so ignorant of what was going on in the world that we would have been quite incapable of thinking such things.

October 22nd

One day when I'm twenty-eight. I sit at my table and there I stay the whole afternoon, unable to write anything. I'm in complete despair and wonder what is to become of me.

At the end of these stagnant hours, my internal voice is perhaps exhausted and has finally fallen silent, my mind is a blank. I'm even feeling very calm and filled with the kind of deep silence that only comes when you've reached this kind of extreme. Suddenly I see myself with absolute clarity. I see what I am. I see my strengths, what I can count on, and I have the conviction that one day I'll be able to write, one day I'll be a writer. But at the same time I see what is holding me back now, and I understand that it will be a long time before I'll be able to free myself, to open myself up to writing.

This is how I had to become aware that I would need to let the years go by while I prepared myself for the task. But how can you resign yourself to waiting when you're burning with impatience, when the need to write is eating into you, when there are bleeding wounds in need of healing through words? I was crushed. I saw clearly that I would only be able to achieve my potential in the last third of my existence. But how would I control my impatience? How could I live through this unbearable waiting? How could I endure such a long period of marking time? I was completely overwhelmed.

October 26th

Sometimes I lie in wait at the spot where thoughts develop themselves, where words are formed, and I try to follow the subtle operations through which wailing shapeless thoughts, struggling to be born, take on a solidity, a structure, and then call up the words which give them existence. (No doubt the way I'm expressing this is open to criticism. There aren't two separate entities, the watcher and the watched. The processes observed by thought happen inside thought itself.)

November 2nd

Yesterday I met a young Flemish woman from Belgium, who speaks French quite well. She's a journalist and has lived in a number of countries in South-East Asia, notably East Timor, during a time of unrest when for Europeans there was a real risk of being killed. I was astonished to learn that she came here with the sole purpose of taking a course in creative writing. She plans to write a book about her schizophrenic brother, based on the journal he keeps and conversations she has with him. I was curious to know what she got out of these classes. It seems that she doesn't learn a great deal. What she really appreciates, and it has nothing to do with the classes she goes to, is the opportunity to work full-time on the book she's started. As we spoke, we discovered that we have a friend in common.

After I left her, I realised that I should have prolonged our meeting. That she wanted to talk longer. She's passionate about writing, about the problems of writing, and there are some things I could have told her. We said goodbye without thinking of exchanging addresses, something I now regret.

This has happened to me on several occasions. I meet a woman I don't know. I talk to her and there is between us a sense of mutual understanding and friendship, but it's only after I've said goodbye that I realise I should have followed up on our meeting.

A moment in time, a silence, an evasive gesture, says Jankelevitch, these are the ways in which the most important things in life choose to make themselves known to us.

April 22nd—Lyons

I'm a long way from Wellington. I will never see the city again, but I still keep its glow inside me, the glow of its street lights, its bays, its skies, the memory of the wind that moans, growls, howls, sometimes night and day.

When it was just a tiny settlement, pioneers came from the four corners of the earth . . . They built roads and houses, then a port, then towers and high-rise buildings. It's been a been a dynamic city for many decades now, and it's still growing to fit its role as capital.

Long before I wandered through its streets, I had been passionately interested in the work of Katherine Mansfield, who died so young and who lived her final years full of nostalgia for the harbour and the hills. Over the five months I spent there, Katherine's voice blended with mine many times, and on several occasions I heard her murmuring to me these words which could be the motto of every writer:

It's only by being faithful to life
that I can be faithful to art
And being faithful to art means
goodness sincerity simplicity integrity

Set here and there into the asphalt footpaths are brass rectangles framing this word and this date, also in metal:

> Shoreline 1840

They mark where the seashore used to be. Then two earthquakes lifted up the ground from beneath the sea, and this Lambton Quay, now one of the central streets, winds between the high-rise buildings a good distance from the waterfront.

The ground shakes all the time and the sea is dangerous. Strong winds, raging seas, unpredictable storms, and over the last two hundred years there's been many a shipwreck at the harbour mouth.

But such dramas and threats cannot crush life.

At rush hour, the streets are filled with a peaceful throng, a mingling of the descendants of the men and women who came here to start a new life. All shapes and sizes, so many different faces, testament to the fact that in the blood that beats in the city's arteries is intermingled the blood of many nations.

Over these five months, the city gave me a great deal, and I'm grateful for this. But when it haunts my thoughts, I can't forget the threat that lurks in the ground and deep beneath it. So, secretly, I say this brief prayer for the city:

Come what may
Stand firm
Stay vibrant
Keep on growing

Translated from the French by Jean Anderson

Part Three

'Tout va bien
à la maison'

Katherine Mansfield
and France

Katherine Mansfield

Katherine Mansfield (1888–1923) not only wrote four of her best-known stories while living in Menton—'The Aloe', 'Bliss', 'Daughters of the Late Colonel' and 'The Stranger'—she also set a number of stories in southern France. Her poetry and journals evoke the mixed emotions of her time in Menton (September 1920–May 1921), during what was largely a period of respite for her. Away from the demands of life in London, she was at last free to do her own writing. Clouding this, though, was the continual upset and difficulty of worsening health. By December 1920, Mansfield was seriously ill and John Middleton Murry joined her in France. In May 1921 she left for Switzerland, in the hope that her health would improve.

Sanary

Her little hot room looked over the bay
Through a stiff palisade of glinting palms
And there she would lie in the heat of the day
Her dark head resting upon her arms
So quiet so still she did not seem
To think or feel or even to dream.

The shimmering blinding web of sea
Hung from the sky and the spider sun
With busy frightening cruelty
Crawled over the sky and spun and spun
She could see it still when she shut her eyes
And the little boats caught in the web like flies.

Down below at this idle hour
Nobody walked in the dusty street
A scent of dying mimosa flower
Lay on the air but sweet—too sweet.

Fleur Adcock

Based in England since 1963, poet Fleur Adcock (born 1934) visited Menton in 1980, when her sister Marilyn Duckworth was the Katherine Mansfield Fellow. Duckworth wrote of the time: 'Menton is truly a small jewel, an exquisite, enchanting place . . . I was grateful for Garavan, for Isola Bella . . . even the funereal smell of pittosporum invading the room was something I could delight in. After dark in June the streets were busy with young people, there was music and dancing on the beach—and once a sword swallower with a nicely oiled torso . . .'

Villa Isola Bella

'You will find Isola Bella in pokerwork on my heart'
—Katherine Mansfield to John Middleton Murry,
10 November 1920 (inscribed outside the
Katherine Mansfield memorial room in Menton)

Your villa, Katherine, but not your room,
and not much of your garden. Goods trains boom
all night, a dozen metres from the bed
where tinier tremors hurtle through my head.
The ghost of your hot flat-iron burns my lung;
my throat's all scorching lumps. I grope among
black laurels and the shadowy date-palm, made
like fans of steel, each rustling frond a blade,
across the gravel to the outside loo
whose light won't wake my sleeping sister. You
smoked shameless Turkish all through your TB.
I drag at Silk Cut filters, duty-free,
then gargle sensibly with Oraldene
and spit pink froth. Not blood: it doesn't mean,
like your spat scarlet, that I'll soon be dead—
merely that pharmacists are fond of red.
I'm hardly sick at all. There's just this fuzz
that blurs and syncopates the singing buzz
of crickets, frogs, and traffic in my ears:

a nameless fever, atavistic fears.
Disease is portable: my bare half-week
down here's hatched no maladie exotique;
I brought my tinglings with me, just as you
brought ragged lungs and work you burned to do;
and, as its fuel, your ecstasy-prone heart.
Whatever haunts my bloodstream didn't start
below your villa, in our genteel den
(till lately a pissoir for passing men).
But your harsh breathing and impatient face,
bright with consumption, must have left a trace
held in the air. Well, Katherine, Goodnight:
let's try to sleep. I'm switching out the light.
Watch me through tepid darkness, wavering back
past leaves and stucco and their reverent plaque
to open what was not in fact your door
and find my narrow mattress on the floor.

Witi Ihimaera

Novelist, short story writer and anthologist Witi Ihimaera (born 1944) has written some of the pivotal books in New Zealand's literary history, among them *Pounamu Pounamu* (1972), *The Matriarch* (1986) and *Bulibasha* (1994). On the hundredth anniversary of Katherine Mansfield's birth, Ihimaera published *Dear Miss Mansfield* (1988), a collection of short stories inspired by Mansfield's writing. Described by the author as a 'token of aroha and respect', the publication was prefaced with a letter to Katherine Mansfield in which Ihimaera writes: 'It is the modern way, Miss Mansfield, for us to have become as much fascinated with your life as with your stories. I myself have always wished to write about your Maori friend Maata and why, if she had indeed possessed a novel you had written, she may have chosen not to part with it. The novella "Maata" is my attempt to provide a Maori response to this question.'

from **Maata**

Mahaki stayed at school another two years. He managed to get his School Certificate and just scraped through his University Entrance. At seventeen he applied for a job on the *New Zealand Herald* in Auckland—and got it. His father wanted him to stay for the shearing, but his mother said 'Go!' There were tears in her eyes as she virtually threw him out the door.

Auckland held Mahaki spellbound. The teeming metropolis seemed to provide everything he had desired. He worked hard at the *Herald* office and played hard at the dances and parties. He made friends with an older journalist, Melvin, and one day, without really knowing why, was compelled to tell him about the red shoes. Melvin, who could be very sarcastic, simply cocked an eye and asked, 'And did you put them on, click your heels three times and think of Kansas?' Mahaki laughed and threw a paper dart at him. 'No,' he answered—and because he saw more sarcasm beginning to form on Melvin's lips said, 'And I didn't dance to my death like Moira Shearer either.' Melvin subsided, obviously disappointed. Then, because he was a clever so-and-so he asked, cunningly, 'They weren't *glass*

152

slippers, perchance?' Mahaki laughed again. 'Anyway,' he explained to Melvin, 'ever since then I've read everything that Katherine Mansfield ever wrote. Everything.'

'Rather you than me, young son,' Melvin said. 'We had to swot "The Fly" at school, in my day, and the wondrous Katherine has ever since been, for me, an ink blot.' Melvin tried to tap a few words on the typewriter and, giving up, took out his pipe and lit it. 'Well, let me know when you read the divine lady's novel,' he said, *and a flash of red danced and dazzled in Mahaki's mind*. 'Novel?' Mahaki asked. 'What novel? I thought she only wrote short stories?' Melvin rolled his eyes to the ceiling and, 'Don't we all?' he murmured, referring to the other reporters in the office, all aspiring to be the next Hemingway. Then he said, 'Actually the novel would really interest you.' He puffed reflectively on his pipe—honestly, Melvin could be so maddening—and continued, 'It's supposed to be about her friend. If the novel exists, that is. Didn't you know? The great Katherine was singularly without good sense or upbringing. She had a *Maori* friend. Maata was her name, I recollect.' Melvin started typing again. 'There's bound to be lots on KM,' he said, 'down in the morgue'—referring to the paper's clippings-files. 'Perhaps there will be something on Maata.' Then his face went red and his stomach began to jiggle. In between his coughing spasms he choked out, 'Ah, ah, Mahaki . . . about your shoe fetish . . . listen, I have these fantastic black high heel pumps at home . . . What say you—' His guffaws echoed throughout the room.

That afternoon, Mahaki visited the newspaper's morgue. Katherine Mansfield had been the first, and perhaps the last, of the great New Zealand short story writers. Forty years after her death in 1923 at Le Prieuré, Fontainebleau, France, her work and life had made her the omnipotent and charismatic presence in New Zealand letters. It was therefore only natural that the newspaper should have such a daunting amount of information about her. The card index was simply the beginning of what would be a long quest.

MANSFIELD, Katherine: Born Kathleen Mansfield
Beauchamp, Wellington, 14 October 1888, at 11 Tinakori

Road, Wellington. Third daughter of Annie Burnell Dyer and Harold Beauchamp, banker (cross index: Beauchamp, Sir Harold). Other siblings: sisters Vera, Charlotte and Jeanne; brother, Leslie, d. France 1915. Attended Karori Village School, 1895–8, Wellington Girls' High School, 1898–9, and Miss Swainson's private school, 1899–1902. Parents took children to England where KM went to Queen's College, Harley Street, London (at 14 years of age) 1903–1906. First published stories in *The Native Companion* (Melbourne) in issues of October–December 1907. For subsequent career see NZ LIT: NZ Writers: Short Stories: Mansfield. Also LIT: UK: Letters of K. Mansfield: Murry.

Nevertheless, as his quest deepened and widened, Mahaki became thoroughly absorbed. Nor could he help but think that seeking as he was 'through the last rubbish can left in the Western world', which was what Melvin called the morgue, only made Katherine Mansfield more real. Every yellowing article, every musty news report reduced the mythical proportion of the person—transformed the goddess into a woman, the icon into a creature of flesh and blood.

And here and there, scattered in the files were photographs of the writer who had formed such a major intersection, historical and theoretical, for New Zealand life and letters. Here, Katherine Mansfield with a capricious glimmer on her lips. Here again, the detested 1913 photograph. Such a modern, *challenging* face! Dark eyes under dark eyebrows, saying 'This is me, like it or lump it, you who stare at me so rudely!' A mouth impatient to open and hair that looked as if it were accustomed to the impetuous toss of the head. A private, knowing face, all the more provocative for that. A face that would be locked away, suffering, into French soil ten years later like a locket in a jeweled box, there to await resurrection and everlasting life at the hand of her husband.

MURRY, John Middleton: Born 6 August 1889, Peckham, London. Impressed by Katherine Mansfield's stories in *New Age* and by her first book 'In A German Pension', published 1911. Met Mansfield in 1912—the love affair, eventual marriage on 3 May 1918, and continuing relationship until

Mansfield's death in 1923, when she was 34, is one of the most famous in literary history. After marriage, Mansfield published her second short story collection, 'Bliss' (1920) and 'The Garden Party' (1922). Murry published two more collections following her death by tuberculosis, as well as her 'Letters' and her 'Journal'. [See NZ LIT: Short Stories: Mansfield, Katherine]

But the achievement? Murry may have had a hand in it, but one only had to look at the *face*. Ah, yes, the face would indeed have remonstrated '*I* did it. *I* did it all. Myself. Me. Katherine. *Kathleen*. Kass. Kezia. Me. *Mansfield*.'

Later that afternoon, as he was finishing, Mahaki came across the paragraph, the resolute sigh, like a credo, which made sense out of that glorious, remote face. 'Here, then, is a little summary of what I need—power, wealth and freedom. It is the hopelessly insipid doctrine that love is the only thing in the world . . . which hampers us so cruelly. We must get rid of that bogey—and then, then comes the opportunity of happiness and freedom.'

Mahaki made further visits to the morgue. Nowhere, however, could he find any references to Maata.

Charles Juliet

Letter to Katherine Mansfield

Lyons
May 2000

It is night, and although you are exhausted, you are unable to sleep. Yesterday you coughed up blood and you cannot stop thinking about death. You are beyond despair, beyond terror. You feel the end is near and you draw on your last ounce of strength to write a few more pages, perhaps one or two short stories to add to those you have already drawn forth from your inner source. This ever more pressing need to write exhausts you at the same time as it strengthens your will to live, your determination to stand firm, to fight to the last breath.

The miracle of words, of literature! You've been gone for several decades, but the collections of short stories and the volumes of correspondence you left for us still speak to us about life and maintain your presence amongst us. And yet, dying at the age of thirty-four, you had so little time to create, and your books take up just a small space on a library shelf. But in writing you were constantly concerned with being true, and inasmuch as truthful words carry within them an inexhaustible energy, you remain for those who appreciate you the companion to whom they love to return.

When I close one or another of your books after rereading a few pages, I am close to you at that hour of night when sleep eludes you. Your wasted body. Your emaciated face. The dark circles under your eyes. The gravity of your expression. The cavernous cough which racks you endlessly and forces you to lay down your pen. You lived through this tragedy far from your father and your sisters, living in New Zealand, far from the man you loved, living in London. At that time, it was thought that the climate in the south of France was beneficial for tuberculosis sufferers, and thus you spent your last years in Menton, Bandol . . . in boarding establishments or rented houses, that is to say in complete solitude. You, who were still young, who loved life so much, who delighted in it down to the tiniest detail, what terrible suffering you had to endure through those days and nights when you felt your strength abandon you, felt that you were slipping inevitably towards the end.

Your final weeks were terrible. Thinking to find help there, perhaps one last, improbable chance of a cure, you had joined the community near Fontainebleau run by Gurdjieff, a man of dubious character. Instead of easing your suffering, they subjected you to unimaginable conditions, thereby hastening your death. Everything seemed to conspire to test you to the utmost, to force you to venture even further up the path that you must climb.

When you decided to leave New Zealand, your birthplace, you went to settle in England, where you lived through uncertain, chaotic times. With no resources, forced to struggle in a world which was new to you and threw you into disarray, where, perhaps led astray by your exuberant energy, you went through many painful experiences. Twice you were deeply affected by bereavement: the death of your much loved young brother, killed in the first months of the Great War, then your mother, struck down by a completely unexpected attack. Then, stricken with tuberculosis, you had to go into exile in France and the need to write became more insistent. Under the impact of these altered circumstances, the woman you were to become would have little in common with the woman you had been. The suffering pulsing inside you sharpened you, wore you away, purified you, so that month after month, year after year, pushing your roots ever deeper, you slowly transformed yourself. In your letters, in your Journal, we see you centre yourself, grow, shine with an ever more radiant light. You lived exactly what you wrote: 'Suffering must become Love.'

Translated from the French by Jean Anderson

Riemke Ensing

Born in the Netherlands in 1939, Riemke Ensing arrived in New Zealand in 1951. In 1988 she composed a suite of poems for the Katherine Mansfield Centenary Conference in Wellington. 'Love Affair' is from the subsequent collection, *The KM File and Other Poems with Katherine Mansfield* (1993). The poem also appears in Ensing's *Talking Pictures; Selected Poems* (2000).

Love Affair

(a given poem from Katherine Mansfield
with thanks to Helen McNeish)

You wrote the table
was laid
for two
but nobody came
so you dined opposite
a white napkin.

It's called giving yourself
to life.
Through the window
a quiet branch
has the evening
to itself
also.

C. K. Stead

from **Mansfield**

**Epilogue
Winter 1918**

She is lying in bed in the Hotel Beau Rivage, hearing the
sea speaking French out there, saying "*issh 'issh*', running up
the sand dropping its aitches. Her shutters are open and she
can see beyond her windows the elegant downward curves
of a single palm tree. It is still quite early in the morning but
people are about, she can hear them speaking to one another
in their forthright—almost harsh—way, *using* their voices,
their throats too, the women especially. Life goes on in France,
but it is changed, it has taken a battering.

   She is half awake, slipping in and out of a dozing dreaming
remembering half-sleep by means of which she is recovering
the past few hectic, exciting and sometimes terrible weeks, the
highs and the lows. She wants to repossess them, add them to
her store. The pile of work she is able to think of as 'good'—
or good enough, publishable—is growing. Of course there
are ideas which fail, stories which somehow 'miss it', and she
doesn't let herself, or them, off lightly; but she feels more in
control now. Her next book will be better than the *German
Pension* collection. After the Woolfs have published *Prelude* as
a book she will think about putting it into a larger collection
with a regular commercial publisher. She is working towards
that. The list of titles is something she jots down in margins
and notebooks and on pieces of blotting paper, playing put
and take as the options increase. That is what she is here for in
Bandol—to recover her health, yes, but also to work.

   The principal scenes of these last weeks play over as in a
movie. She sees herself taking a turn on the ferry deck before
retiring, standing at the rail feeling as if she is on a mythic
journey again, the ship sailing into the softness of a snowstorm.

She is shivering, but she has eaten a big supper—such a *whack* of beef, with bread and butter and tea. The snowflakes flutter like moths in the ship's lights, catching fire there and taking it down with them on to the dark heaving glossy-animal flank of the sea.

Then there was the day in Le Havre and the journey to Paris, revealing that though the 'War to end War' could put the heating out of action on the SNCF, slow its trains, make a joke of its timetables, and allow snow to come sneaking in without a ticket through its broken windows, it could make no impact at all on the glories of French bread or French cheeses.

The next day was Paris, making her way '*comme un poulet malade*'—like a sick chicken on the icy pavements, having her visa stamped, trying to send messages, get money, arrange that she and her luggage should arrive at the same place, discover to which train at what time on which platform she should change at Marseilles—all of this done, so to speak, against the odds, against the grain of the war, and yet through it all finding herself simply loving France and the French and the French language. It must have been (she tells herself now) some kind of saintly madness bestowed on her by the fact of being at last on the move, let out of her cage, relieved of the boredom of illness—so she was seeing, not quite 'France and the French', but a mirror, a reflection of her own unreasonable, unseasonable happiness.

It couldn't last of course, and didn't. She was not well enough, and the way ahead was too tough. The long delays, the uncertainties, the cold, dirt and discomfort of the train, the lack of food, hot drinks, pillows, working wash-rooms—all of that together with the aching-and-burning in her lung that got worse by the hour . . . And then, late in the long cold night, somewhere south of Lyons as the train crawled through the blacked-out landscape, two French women talking about the Mediterranean coast, agreeing that the popular idea that it was good for people with damaged lungs was a myth, and surely contradicted by the facts. The Protestant cemeteries down there (did nobody notice?) were full of English, Germans, Scandinavians, who had come south to get better and had only dug their own graves. It was something in the air . . . Something fatal . . . They didn't stand a chance . . . One had known an American girl, beautiful, suffering only from bronchitis, expected to get better in three months, hadn't lasted six weeks . . .

It was all in French, in an undertone, but she heard it and understood it as clearly as if it had been a bell tolling distantly but getting nearer as the hours passed and the train closed on that fatal coast. She tried to dismiss them from her mind, joke them out of existence. Bubble bubble toil and trouble. Where's your sister, Sisters? Missed the train, did she?

She dropped back again into an exhausted sleep, but took them with her there, still talking about lungs and death and the graveyards of the Côte d'Azur.

Then came Marseilles, the effort of it, the gathering of her luggage, the long queues, getting her visa stamped again, the uncertainty about where from, and when, the train to Bandol would leave, the bruising rushes with the crowd as announcements and contradictions sent it surging from one platform to another . . .

Simply to be on board, seated, with a compartment all to herself, as it turned out to be, and to hear the doors banging shut and the whistle blowing, was such a relief it almost cancelled the disappointment she felt at having eight Serbian officers and their two dogs push in with her at the last moment.

'Madame does not object?' one asked in French, bowing and baring a set of exceptionally white teeth under his black moustache.

She felt it would not have made any difference if Madame had; and in any case they were handsome animals, all ten of them, and, ill or not, this side of death she was not going to be indifferent to manly good looks. 'Not at all,' she assured him. 'More bodies means more warmth, *n'est-ce pas?*'

In their own language they discussed what this meant, seemed to come to an understanding, and all smiled at her together. Even the dogs smiled. She felt she had recruited a palace guard. It was a piece of good fortune. The train was not moving, despite a second whistle-blast from the guard and a wave of his flag. Out there on the platform a contingent of French soldiers were holding up the departure, demanding places on the train. The shouting grew louder. All at once they attacked. It was no outburst of good-humoured high jinks. These were angry men just back from the war zone around Verdun, bitter at what they had been put through while these civilians had sat at home. Why did people need to travel while there was a war on? Were they going on holiday?

They burst into the train, shouting, dragging passengers, men and women, old and young, man-handling them out on to the platform and taking their places. The Serbians were ordered out but refused. They too were fighting men, they insisted. They had been fighting for France, and had earned their places in blood. Coriolanus-like, they uncovered their scars. They were staunch, determined. Also, they were armed.

'Well, *she* must go,' a French soldier said, grabbing Katherine and dragging her towards the door.

The Serbian who had first spoken to her intervened, holding the Frenchman by the shoulder, towering over him. '*Non, Monsieur. Elle est ma femme.*'

The Frenchman, who smelled strongly of wine, tobacco and stale sweat, hesitated, then let her go. He didn't know whether to believe it, but it might be true (she was foreigner), and clearly it would have been folly to intervene between such a large man and his wife. The Serbians eased him out of the compartment and secured the door with their dogs' leather collars. As the train began to move she could see civilians, some weeping, others angry and bruised, some with the luggage and some with nothing, all helpless on the platform. Up and down the train the French soldiers burst into a triumphant 'Marseillaise'.

She had been frowning hard, concentrating on the thought that whatever happened she must not cry. Now she smiled at her protector.

'Thank you,' she said. '*Merci beaucoup, Monsieur. Danke schön.*' And then, searching among the bits and pieces of several languages she'd learned in Germany, she added, not feeling quite sure it was the word she wanted, '*Hvala!*'

They laughed and applauded. 'My wife is a linguist,' he

     The Colour of Distance

said in French. 'Madame is welcome. Now she will have a small brandy and a cigarette?'

Bandol, when she'd reached it at last, she found changed by war and weather. At the Beau Rivage the management were new, there was no heating, the service was skimpy, the food basic and the prices high. There were few guests; its verandahs and pale public rooms with their white cane furniture seemed empty and battened down like a ship in a gale, whispering and gasping with sudden gusts and draughts. She had to buy wood for the fireplace in her room. In the town she was not immediately recognised by shopkeepers who had been her friends. When she reminded them who she was they told her, with a combination of kindness and frankness alien to the Anglo-Saxon, that she was *changed*, that it was clear she'd been unwell, that she'd lost her pretty-girl look.

She found herself homesick alternatively grieving for Freddie and missing Jack, loving them both in a way that seemed wild, extravagant. Every day she wrote to Jack; every day she looked out for his replies and felt panicky and bereft if none came. But she was working. The weather improved. And the maid, Juliette, who had little to do in this lean time, was the rare kind of being whose good humour and goodwill could make it seem the sun was shining even when it wasn't.

The sea out there is still speaking French under its breath. '*'isshsh*' it says to the sand, '*'isshsh.*' She slips in and out of sleep, but the sound stays with her. She knows where she is. The recollections that come to her are real, are dreams, are real again. Leslie, still a small boy, is playing with the cat on the floor beside her bed. Her mother sits fanning herself in a white basket chair with a pink cushion on the hotel verandah. Her father is the man at the bar-tabac along the seafront, speaking excellent French. Now Fred is standing at the window, looking out at the sea and laughing. But these surprises force her awake again.

She is remembering the day, soon after settling in at the Beau Rivage, when she decided she would visit Madame Allegre. She went up from the seafront, away from the shops and cafés, turning on to the gravel road that climbed steeply above and beyond the town. There was the sea coming into view again away to her right. She passed the olive grove, its trees blown silver in the wind, and the grassy field that had been their short-cut to the market. She passed the wall where they had seen 'the last lizard of summer' sunning itself. There were tiny puffs of yellow blossom on the feathery grey-green mimosa. Now she could see the Villa Pauline up ahead, pink, looking over its own wall towards her. For a moment the greyness of the day made no difference. She saw it as it had been on the good days; as it had been when the weather had meant next to nothing—when every day, warm or cold, wet or dry, had been good.

She stopped because something was happening to her. At first she thought she must be ill, it was so strong; and then recognised that it wasn't physical. What she was feeling was an emotion. Regret? Nostalgia? No single word quite described it because it involved pleasure as well as pain. Intensity. Something of the mind but so powerful it was felt in the body, at the fingertips and in the nerve ends; in the scalp and at the throat. Her life and Jack's met and were joined for ever at this point, in this place. Robert Louis Stevenson, she remembered, had written, 'Happy? I was happy once. That was in Hyères.' Why did it only occur to her now that Hyères was just along the coast, and that they—she and Jack—could write the same of Bandol?

She pushed open the gate and heard its familiar creak, and the crunch of the gravel under her feet. It was strange how so many gates and doors had voices as distinct as a human voice. If she'd been blind, brought here from anywhere on earth and asked where she was, hearing that sound she could have answered correctly without a moment's pause.

She walked up the path past the almond tree and up the steps to the door which was slightly ajar. She knocked, pushed it open (it stuck, as always), and was greeted by Madame Allegre who was airing the house, getting it ready to let again when the spring arrived. The greeting, once she'd been recognised, was fulsome, noisy. The kisses went from cheek to cheek and back again, as if she were a tennis match. She was peered at, reviewed, kissed again, led indoors. They sat on either side

The Colour of Distance

of the table where she'd worked on 'The Aloe'. They talked about the war, the great battles now starting up again; about the weather, about Jack in London, and the Allegres' son who was wounded—thank God, because he wouldn't have to fight any more.

Through all of this, and especially when she saw her own photograph still on the shelf where Jack had propped it, it was as if she were holding her breath, fighting back tears at the knowledge that something invaluable had been cast aside, casually, and could never be recovered.

The tears didn't come until she was walking down the hill again. Rain had started to fall, a light misty shower blown in from the sea, and she said over to herself

> Il pleure dans mon coeur
> Comme il pleut sur la ville.

Back on the waterfront she leaned over the wall looking at the grey sea and watching North African soldiers kicking something about on the sand. She thought of it, that soft object doing service for a football, as herself, kicked about by Fate. It was a bad moment, a moment of self-pity, and she went into combat with it. Whatever was left behind when she and Jack answered Lawrence's summons, the decision, she knew, had been as much hers as his. And self-reproach was no use. It had to do with what was called 'free will'. She had never thought of her will (though she knew she had one) as 'free'. Decisions of that kind were not 'choices'. They were just events, happenings. They were what you found yourself *doing*, in the circumstances, being the person you were. If you had been another person you might have done different, but you were not.

So the best had to be made of whatever was the case; and if the moment ever came when regret and nostalgia seemed to be taking control, then it was time to remember Freddie's advice: burn your boats every morning; live, not as if there were no tomorrow, but as if there were no yesterday.

She has arranged her days into a routine which allows plenty of rest, a certain amount of walking, and some hours of work. Her best hours for writing are after her mid-afternoon walk and before dinner. She has written a long story about the French and the English, told by a Frenchman, a writer—partly Carco. She began it as an exposure of this character's corruption and cynicism and, day by day, wrote herself into his voice, into his consciousness, until she ended up *being* him, enjoying him, liking him. There is an Englishman in the story, based partly on Jack (at least he has Jack's rolling gait and some of his mannerisms). And there is an Englishwoman called Mouse, a pale shadow of herself, who in a crisis says very little and demands *tea*. It is so new in technique and content she feels everything that comes after must take it into account or seem a step backward. She has also dreamed a small story, even its name, 'Sun and Moon', and next day written it straight down. And now she's writing another—about London, middle-class marriage, infidelity.

The weather which began so bleak and cold has changed in a way the locals tell her is characteristic of the region: one moment winter, with cold wind and rain, the next a sky and a sea like silk, the mimosa exploding into gold, jonquils yellow and white everywhere, windows and doors wide open, a smile on every face that says, even if no word is uttered, '*Fait beau, n'est-ce pas?*'

There are shadows, of course: her fears; the difficulty of sleeping through the night when she is writing; her anxiety about Jack in London; the burn in her creaking lung and the uncertainty about what it might mean . . . And now there is Ida, the Rhodesian Mountain, who has fought her way past every obstacle, every wartime restriction on travel, and come hurtling south convinced by some ghoulish intuition that she is needed. Katherine is hating her at this moment—unreasonably, she knows, and therefore holding her hatred in check. The woman loves her; wants to eat her alive; is disappointed (or so Katherine persuades herself) that her darling is not worse, seriously ill, dying, so she would be needed *really*. Since she can't eat her friend she eats everything else (they take meals together) in amounts that seem to Katherine excessive, even

The Colour of Distance

disgusting. Ida is submissive but also single-minded, focused, determined. It is a war, Katherine tells herself (everything is war!), in which Ida's strongest weapon is the guilt her devotion and subjugation cause Katherine to feel.

Katherine is trying not to be cruel. This means she *has* been cruel, but not as she might have been if she did not put a brake on herself. She knows Ida will help her get back to London when the weather is warmer. That will be fortunate; even perhaps necessary, if the expected spring offensive occurs and there are long delays on the trains and interruptions to the journey. So she will make use of Ida, as she has done in the past—and should be grateful, shouldn't she? She thinks not. She should acknowledge Ida's devotion, and does, but at this moment she can't think of it as other than a burden, an imposition, and Ida as the leech on her life.

She's not well. She has not had her Aunt Martha since leaving England and would love to believe (remembering that Sunday afternoon in bed with Jack before her departure) that she is pregnant. But she doesn't believe it. There are none of the other signs (sore breasts, vomiting) she remembers from the far-off pregnancy that ended with so much blood and unhappiness in Worishofen.

She must take comfort in her work. It's what matters now in her life—that and her love for Jack. There is nothing else. Her new story has kept her awake last night, suffering a kind of nervous excitement at the thought of what may happen when her second book is published, the success it may bring.

She must get up now, have breakfast, begin. She remembers lines she learned at school from Shakespeare's *Venus and Adonis*, and says them over to herself:

Lo, here the gentle lark, wary of rest,
From his moist cabinet mounts up on high,
And wakes the morning from whose silver breast
The sun ariseth in his majesty;
   Who doth the world so gloriously behold,
   That cedar-tops and hills seem burnish'd gold.

In a rush of energy she throws back the bedclothes, jumps from the bed and runs three steps to the window. It causes her to cough, deep in her lungs—a coughing fit that drives her backward to the edge of the bed where she collapses for a moment, recovering. Something tastes strange. She puts her hand to her mouth. There is blood. Not just a fleck or spot. A lot—a bright thick smear of it across and between her fingers.

There is something she remembers now. On that last quick dash to Garsington she picked up Colvin's life of Keats which Jack had borrowed from Ottoline. She sat on his bed skimming it for an hour or more. One thing that stuck in her mind was Keats noting the bright red blood—arterial blood—of his first haemorrhage, and saying he knew what it was, and that it would be fatal, because he'd seen it in the case of his brother. He knew it was his death warrant.

That is the colour Katherine sees on her hand, and goes on seeing as it creeps through her fingers. The seconds tick by, and the minutes. There is no great rush of blood, but nor is it the merest trace. She coughs and it is still there. She remains sitting on the bed. She thinks of Chekhov. She was always too close to him in her imagination—borrowed his style in her earliest work, even pinched a story from him. Is she now going to die his death? What would that be? A punishment? Or just an ordinary old irony?

After a time there is only a very faint trace—but she knows this is not an end. It is a beginning. Why else has there been that burning sensation? And Dr Ainger speaking of a 'spot' or 'shadow'? At the time she let her mind slide over it. Pulled the blind down on it.

This is tuberculosis. Has to be.

She is calm. There is a fear so deep—much deeper than panic—that dulls and anaesthetises; that simply waits for the worst to happen. It must, she supposes, be what a person feels being led to execution. She was told that her brother's wounds were too terrible for him to feel pain. She guesses there must be a parallel protection against fear. When you *know* you are going to die perhaps you are beyond fear. Perhaps you only fear when your death is less than certain, or when you can't believe in it.

The Colour of Distance

I must work, is what she tells herself. The book must be finished, and perhaps (this kind of dying sometimes takes several years) there will be another. If I have to go (she's remembering Fred's resolve not to argue with his fate) I'll go quietly—but not quickly, and I will leave my fingerprints on things.

She goes to the window again and looks out. She closes her eyes and summons Wellington Harbour, and the hills behind it, and the sea beyond. They are there. She can count on them. They will always be there.

She opens her eyes and sees Bandol. It too is there—the town, the port, the Mediterranean all blue and turquoise in the morning light. There are three fishing boats being mended and tarred under her window, and one getting a new coat of paint. Not far from the shore fishermen are out in pairs in their smallest boats. One sculls lightly, little flicks of the oars, so the boat inches over the water. The other stands in the prow with a spear, waiting to strike.

She notices that the two submarines have gone from the harbour; have crept out at night to do their underwater work. The destroyer is showing signs of getting up steam. Death must go on.

She will have to find a way to break this news to Jack. That will take a very careful choice of words. Yes, for words on the page, she *does* consider herself responsible. *Those* are her acts of will!

But first, she had better have breakfast.

Katherine Mansfield

from **Letters and Journals**

To John Middleton Murry
(19 September 1920)
As to the weather it is really heavenly weather. It is too hot for any exertion, but a breeze lifts at night, and I can't tell you what scents it brings, the smell of a full summer sea and the bay tree in the garden and the smell of lemons. After lunch today we had a sudden tremendous thunderstorm, the drops of rain were as big as marguerite daisies—the sky was all glittering with broken light—the sun a huge splash of silver. The drops were like silver *fishes* hanging from the trees. I drank the rain from the peach leaves and then pulled a shower bath over my head. Every violet leaf was full. I thought of you—these are the things I want you to have. Already one is conscious of the whole sky again and the light on the water. Already one listens for the grasshopper's fiddle, one looks for the tiny frogs on the path—one watches the lizards . . . I feel so strangely as though I were the one who is home and you are away. I long for you here.

(27 September 1920)
The lizards here *abound*. There is one big fellow, a perfect miniature crocodile, who lurks under the leaves that climb over a corner of the terrace. I watched him come forth today—*very* slithy—and eat an ant. You should have seen the little jaws, the flick flick of the tongue, the great rippling pulse just below the shoulder. His eyes, too. He listened with them—and when he couldn't find another ant, he stamped his front paw—and then, seeing that I was watching, *deliberately* winked, and slithered away.

There is also a wasps' nest in the garden. Two infant wasps came out this morning and each caught hold of a side of a *leaf* and began to tug. It was a brown leaf the size of three tea leaves. They became furious. They whimpered, whiney-pined—snatched at each other—wouldn't give way and finally one *rolled* over and couldn't roll back again—just lay there kicking. I never saw such a thing. His twin then couldn't move the leaf at all. I pointed out the hideous moral to my invisible playmate.

(4 October 1920)

. . . *Whatever* my feelings are, I am *not* justified in giving way to them before you or in letting you see even the shadow of the border of that shadowy country that we exiles from health inhabit. It is not fair. So I'm resolute that you shan't be plagued again, my dearest darling, and determined to keep my resolution. Help me to.

I'm sending you and Milne a dozen kāhki (I don't know how to spell it: that's phonetic) to eat for your breakfasts. They are very good and very healthy. I send them unripe. You must wait until they are soft, then cut off the top, squeeze a *lot* of lemon-juice inside and eat with a teaspoon. Perhaps they won't be a treat, after all. I always long to *send* you things. Please give my love to Milne. He sounds so nice in the house. I wonder what Wing thinks of the clarinet.

Walpole's novel which I mean to do for next week (1 col) ought to be a very good prop to hang those very ideas on that I tried to communicate to you. I want to take it seriously and really say why it fails—for, of course, it does fail. But his 'intention' was serious. I hope I'll be able to say what I do mean. I am *no* critic of the homely kind. 'If you would only explain quietly in simple language,' as L. M. said to me yesterday. Good Heavens, that *is* out of my power.

The garden menagerie includes snakes—a big chap as thick as my wrist, as long as my arm, slithered along the path this morning and melted into the bushes. It wasn't horrid or fearful, however. As to the mice—Marie's piège seems to snap in the most revolting way. A fat one was offered to a marauding cat at the back door yesterday, but it *refused* it. 'Polisson! Tu veux un morceau de sucre avec?' I heard Marie scold. She is very down on the cats here; she says they are malgracieux.

Katherine Mansfield

I feel this letter is cold and poor; the fruit is not good to eat. It's rather like that withered fig tree. Do you know there is a kind of fig tree which is supposed to be of the family of that unfortunate one—it is dark stemmed and its leaves are black, they flap on the blackened boughs, they are like leaves that a flame has passed over. *Terrible.* I saw one once in a valley, a beautiful valley with a river flowing through it. There was linen drying on the banks and the women were beating the water and calling to one another—gaily—and there was this *sad* tree. L. M. who was with me said 'Of course the *explanation* is that one must never cease from giving'. The fig tree has no figs—so Christ cursed it. *Did you ever!* There's such a story buried under the whole thing—isn't there—if only one could dig it out . . .

(5 October 1920)
. . . The Journal—I have absolutely given up. I dare not keep a journal. I should always be trying to tell the truth. As a matter of fact I dare not tell the truth. I feel I *must* not. The only way to exist is to go on and try and lose oneself—to get as far as possible away from *this* moment. Once I can do that all will be well. So it's stories or nothing. I expect I shall kick off soon— perhaps today. Who knows? In the meantime I peg away too, darling, in my fashion . . .

Journal

(October 1920)
'What about a cauliflower?' I said. 'A cauliflower with white sauce.'

'But they are so dear, Madame,' wailed Marie. 'So dear. One little cauliflower for 2fr.50. It's robbery, it's . . .'

Suddenly through the kitchen window I saw the moon. It was so marvellously beautiful that I walked out of the kitchen door, through the garden and leaned over the gate before I knew what I was doing. The cold bars of the gate stopped me. The moon was full, transparent, glittering. It hung over the sighing sea. I looked at it for a long time. Then I turned round, and the little house faced me—a little white house quivering with light, a house like a candle shining behind a feather of mimosa-tree. I had utterly forgotten these things when I was ordering the dinner. I went back to the kitchen.

'Let us have a cauliflower at any price,' I said firmly.

And Marie muttered, bending over a pot—*could* she have understood?—'*En effet*, the times are dangerous!'

Journal

(December 1920)

Oh Life! Accept me—make me worthy—teach me.

I write that. I look up. The leaves move in the garden, the sky is pale, and I catch myself weeping. It is hard—it is hard to make a good death . . .

*

To the Hon. Dorothy Brett

(20 April 1921)

. . . Here it is so cold that it might be November. We are both frozen, we shiver all day. I get up from 11–5.30 and turn the clock round so as to get back to bed more quickly. I've been spitting blood since last Tuesday too—which is horrid. It makes one feel that while one sits at the window the house is on fire. And the servants have gone mad or bad or both. One has completely disappeared, only her feather duster remains. She wasn't a little one either. But I expect we shall come across her one day. I have a fancy she is in one of the chimneys. All our flags are pinned on Switzerland. Meadows, trees, mountains, and kind air. I hope we shall get there in time . . .

Katherine Mansfield 173

Part Four

A Nice Place
on the Riviera

Allen Curnow

During his tenure as Katherine Mansfield fellow in 1983, Allen Curnow (1911–2001) wrote 'Gare SNCF Garavan', which appeared in *The Loop in Lone Kauri Rd* (1986). The Garavan train station is located about fifty metres from the Mansfield Room in the Villa Isola Bella and the tracks pass a few metres in front of the room. Curnow's last collection, *The Bells of Saint Babels* (2001), contains the extended meditation on the Côte d'Azur, Pascal and other matters French, 'A Nice Place on the Riviera'.

Gare SNCF Garavan

The day doesn't come to the boil, it guards
a banked-up flame under a cool first light.
Madame tethers her Siamese to the doorway
of the Gare SNCF, the shadier side
of the tracks where we mustn't stray.

The tracks are bare, the pines don't stir, the haze
is international, Cap Martin is a thing
in the mind's eye of 'that eternal sea',
Bordighera just one more. Behind the doorway
of the sanctuary, something rings, Madame is

answering. I am questioning a blossom of
some nameless yellow creeper about the excitements
of life on a warm wall. Pussy is overweight,
so is Madame, but active, panties and *collants*
hang from an upper room, over the yard side

of the Gare, the seaward, shaded by the dark
eyelashes of the pines in a light that is not
explicit. Landward the Alpes Maritimes lean
scarily steep-to, by the Gare clock
I can relax, nobody's yet begun saying

'to the mountains, fall on us', only indistinct
voices drop from the lemon-gardens, the villas.
A frequent service. Madame emerges, bearing her
official baton, producing a train from Nice,
Italy's minutes away, an old-fashioned thought,

an old-fashioned iron expostulation of
wheels, fluttering doors, interrupts nothing.
So much at risk, a miracle that so much gets
taken care of, Madame picks up her cat from
the *quai* and cuddles it, conversing with friends.

Menton, London
1983

A Nice Place on the Riviera

The last act is bloody, however fine the rest of the play.
They throw earth over your head and it is finished for ever.
Pascal, *Pensées*, XII.210 *(tr. A.J. Krailsheimer).*

I
Refuge in San
Remo won't work

out. Local health
officialdom rules

La signora è
malata. Not

welcome this side
of the frontier.

France is not far:
why don't I try

cousin Connie
Beauchamp? Nice place

they say they've got
in Menton. She

and inseparable
Jinnie Fullerton.

This horrible cough!
Kind souls. Perhaps

their prayers will work
with a few more Hail

Marys thrown in.
Connie or Jinnie

(never mind which)
murmured 'The Lord

has delivered you
into our hands'.

2
'No personal God
or any such

nonsense'—Katherine
Mansfield Beauchamp

to Murry, spouse,
from Villa Isola

Bella, Menton,
18 October

being much the age
Blaise Pascal was

Allen Curnow   179

(three centuries
back) to whom God

personally did
appear that day

'from about ten
thirty p.m.

till past midnight'.
Sick too. And wrote

'Fire', 'Jesus', 'God'
(ten times over) *and*

much more. They found
the parchment stitched

into his clothes
when they stripped him for

burial. Not known
like her, at this

address.

3
     And there's
his *Pensées*, where

I left the book,
this rickety desk,

the Villa's one
spare room, kept up

in her name. Here
the annual New

Zealander sweats
brief tenure out,

memorialising
her genius. I

brought profound Blaise
along, whose death-

mask eyeballs me
glazedly, from

the paperback's
cover, with eyes

they plucked I (learn)
out of his painted

portrait and poked
them in here

and they look it.

4
Spring equinox:
lemon trees drenched

one minute, next
blast of the same

black sirocco
blow-dries bright green

under the shuttered
villa windows. Miss

Fullerton rose
from the escritoire,

Allen Curnow

having inscribed
her gift, the book,

from Jinnie, to
Katie, Saint

Joseph's day, nine-
teen twenty, *The*

*Imitation of
Christ* (Thomas à

Kempis) in soft
red morocco,

title in gilt . . .
One Turkey rug's

length separates
the two. The *bonne*

brings coffee, liqueur.
That rabid wind

bangs shutters, dis-
colours the sea,

dishevels the world
outdoors. Beside

the demitasses
the Abdullahs in

their silver box,
the *Imitation*

waits to be read . . .
The climate here's

her only hope,
some doctor said.

Always a chance.

5
Your call, says Blaise.
Heads, there's God;

Tails, none. The coin
infinitely far

away spins itself
asleep, a still

spherical blur—
slowing, splits down

meridians, falls
over, face down,

face up. Your call.
God knows the odds

incalculably. Tell
me what your plans

are, for retirement.

6
Pieces of his mind
by the thousand,

jottings on jumbo-
size sheets. Pierced

for threading string.
Tied in *liasses*.

Allen Curnow   183

Too sick, or just
ran out of time

sorting the huge
heap. Such heads as

PROOFS OF JESUS
NATURE CORRUPT,

SO ARE WE ALL,
CAUSES, EFFECTS . . .

7
Imitation—big
ask—of the life

he lived, the death
he died—if that

doesn't make two
of us, there's one

Christ lookalike
more than we knew.

8
Top-heavy *Alpes
Maritimes* grind

the sky small. Fast
forward, to autumn.

One of those two
women, who could

be seen watchfully
to cross the rail

tracks where they start
threading the rock

through to Liguria
halts, chestily coughs

in her handkerchief:
but has finished

writing her last
storybook; by now

consumption's two
years' gallop away

from Gurdjieff's
Institute, that

fatal torrential
haemorrhage, at

Fontainebleau,
stumbling upstairs.

9
Fast forward again
top-heavy *Alpes*

Maritimes grind
the sky small. One

more dull day scraped
off a slaty sea.

Nigel Cox

Nigel Cox (born 1951) is the author of five novels. In 1991, he held the Katherine Mansfield Memorial Fellowship, and later published 'When I Was a Writer' in the literary magazine *Sport*. Based in Berlin from 2000 to 2005, Cox led the project team which created the Jewish Museum Berlin, and was Head of Exhibitions and Education until his return to New Zealand.

When I Was a Writer

The Katherine Mansfield Room is a sort of above-ground cellar beneath the terrace of the Villa Isola Bella where Katherine lived for a few months in 1920–1. A photograph in Gillian Boddy's book about her shows her on the terrace but she was very ill at that time, scarcely mobile, according to the one handed-down eye-witness report I've had of her, and I suspect she never descended to this spare room, this sleep-out—so was KM ever in the KM Room? But it's a good place to work; there's a sense that work is all that's ever been done within its thick creamy walls, which keep out France, and the sound of the trains, and the heat, even when it's not hot outside.

Inside it the Fellow tries to ignore the ghosts (did Janet Frame sit facing this window or that one?) and get on with justifying the grant ($36,000, to cover travel, accommodation and living—Anne, Anneli and I will make it stretch 8 1/2 months if we're careful). This Fellow has a work chart to keep him honest; so far it's a five-day week, from 8 in the morning till somewhere between 4.30 and 6pm, with on average half an hour for lunch. There's no phone calls, no visitors, no interruptions, so you get on with it (how's that, Mr McLauchlan?*). I've never really had an extended stretch of being able to write all day before; it's *tiring*.

* When Gordon McLauchlan's attack on state patronage of writers was published in the *NZ Herald* at least half a dozen 'friends' instantly thought of me and sent a copy. For two weeks afterwards I worked in a fury of self-justifying indignation.

186

Every morning I come across town on the train, walk under the railbridge and, avoiding the dogs', which is *everywhere*, make the short climb up the av. Katherine Mansfield to the Room. About a week ago I heard a hissing in the stone wall outside the gate to the Room's garden. A small pipe appeared to have sprung a leak within the wall; a dark trickle ran down the white of the 'ancient stones' and away along the gently sloping earth gutter. Your novelist, ever alert for a Real Story, followed the trickle ('This is your work!'), but became worried in case someone saw and thought him soft in the head.

For the next week when I turned up each morning, there was the trickle. After three days a clematis-like vine, enjoying the water, produced two bright yellow flowers. 'Voilà!' I said in my excellent French. Inside the Room I pressed on with the masterwork.

Then two days ago workmen arrived, six of them, from the Menton council, to clear the ground of any weeds, overhanging branches or rubbish. Everywhere in the city you can see the big clean-up in progress; August is coming and an immaculate Menton justifies the this-month-only inflation of prices. Menton (pop. 25,000) attends to presentation: the by-laws say you can paint your house any colour you like as long as it's terracotta. In my tiny garden the workmen remove all extraneous vegetable matter very efficiently, which I regret; urban France seems to be without backyards—our apartment has no 'outside'—and I rather like the little jungle at my back door. Then . . . and here's the question . . . did those workmen inform the water board there was a leak? Or is water usage in this town so carefully monitored that one of their dials told them they were losing precious drops? The latter isn't hard to imagine: this is a nation of dial-watchers, schedule-keepers and form-fillers, and France has had low rainfall for three years. The whole of Europe is short of water, I read, except (of course) England. Whatever: that afternoon the water-men arrived. I keep the gate to the Room's garden locked to deter the KM fans; I hurried out with the key. The workmen and I quickly established that we didn't have a language in common, and that I didn't know where the key to the stopcock on my end of the pipe was, and that I hadn't fiddled with it (honest!) and that, well, it was their business. This exchange had in it everything that a writer hates: failure in the language department, failure in the fixit department (okay, a male writer), a distraction from work that's not fascinating (let me rephrase that). They thrashed around in the bushes out there while I thrashed around in the bushes in here. Finally they shouted to me, 'Ay!' and the foreman asked with his hands, is there a telephone in there? 'No. Non.' He called me, 'Puta!' which I didn't go for all that much (though it's Spanish, isn't it? I searched for his mantilla), but I could see him thinking, That effete creature is worried I'm going to get my dirty boots all over his invaluable manuscript. I explained that there wasn't a phone—this is a writer's room—and then remembered for him that there's a cardphone at 'la gare'. He repeated the word, correcting my pronunciation, then off they went. They were back shortly with a huge spanner, which they took into the bushes—by then I was back to work and didn't watch—and departed. Later I discovered the Room's water had been cut off: no coffee, no toilet.

I waited a day, seeing if doing nothing would help, carefully recalling what had happened in minute detail. Away from home and without subtlety in the language of the country you're in, *real encounters with the locals* are rare, these microscopic incidents loom large.

I didn't want to start going to cafés for coffee, was quite soon peeing into very yellow toilet water. At lunchtime I assembled a letter, in French, for the General Secretary of the council here, M. Kettela, who is responsible for the Room; he speaks no English. I always write any complicated messages out and pass them to people to read (this is true even when I'm in New Zealand: writers trust writing) and it was fun getting the exact words for 'outside tap' and conjugating the verbs. Then, not wanting to be a bother, I decided I should try Direct Action first and checked all the manholes and small access hatches, searching for the toby. Looking around the garden, I realised these hatches were everywhere, I found ten in as many square metres. They were slightly scarey to open—I don't go much on big black spiders running up my bare arms, and I'm not sure if there's snakes around here. (At this point I remember that once, in Greece, needing a boulder to anchor a flysheet, I seized a hefty one and uncovered a nest of scorpions, one of them still on the boulder: *squash!*) The hatches gave access to beautifully maintained storm water pipes, all empty. There's something eerie about pipes that you can't see up: their hollow sound, the sense that any moment something might gush from them. These were part of such a complicated network. I thought about French organisation, which can be very impressive, and their determination to have things the way they want. To my relief the pipes had no occupants to face down, though when I opened the meterbox something rattled like a rat in behind its base-board. Then a large green lizard shot across the dials and disappeared behind the board again. I'm fond of lizards, they're always beautiful in colour, and I closed the door carefully. One day, checking the Room's mailbox (which I do obsessively about six times a day—so far it's yielded just one aerogramme), I found I'd squashed a tiny lizard, about an inch and a half long, faintly reminiscent of a tuatara, though this one, in death, was pale grey. It'd crawled in through the mail slot and then got caught in the hinge when I closed the box. These little everyday tragedies can make you feel desperate when you're away; there's no familiar for them to be absorbed into. It was another lizard that helped me feel at home here. This was a month ago, on the first really sunny day. The colours all changed and became soft, everything looked warm and sleepy in the steady light (Brian Boyd—Nabokov lived here—says, 'orange-palmy-blue Menton', which gives the feeling exactly) and as I came under the railway bridge something rattled in the stone wall. I stopped, waited, and a beautiful lizard slowly extruded itself from a hole the power board had drilled to run cable into. It came out into the sun, blackgreen, with hidden lights among the stickles on its back and the red of toadstools on the undersides of its footpads. I felt at home because after that the lizard was something I looked for every morning. Fauna that's exotic (to you) seems to tell you you're in another country. I mean, all these French people could *fly* south, settle in New Zealand and learn to eat our lumpen food, but animals, reptiles especially, don't become ubiquitous easily.

Because I can't speak the language I seem to be paying great attention in this country to the natural world. But it frustrates me; there seems no way to identify the birds whose calls I hear outside as I work—so how will I write about them?

Late that afternoon I visited the Mairie, which is the mayor's nest, the Town Hall, armed with my carefully compiled letter. In Menton the Mairie is a beautiful building, formal, modest in its dignity (terracotta, of course), with a huge, clean tricoleur, and tall, highly polished wooden doors. It houses the council offices, and the local Salle de Mariage, in which you must, if you wed in France, be married. This particular Salle was designed by Jean Cocteau in 1957; it's hard to imagine anything like it being allowed in New Zealand. The chamber itself is not vast but the symbolic figures Cocteau painted on the walls and ceiling are too big for the space, so that you seem to cower beneath them: prancing outlines, pale green, ochre, faintly erotic, their stylised perfection mocking the everyday creatures who are marrying beneath them. Under your feet the carpet is royal red, spread with imitation leopard skins. A thin light rises from black, diamond-shaped shades held at head-height by metal vines which climb, writhing, from the floor . . .

I'd been to the Mairie a few times and now approached it with caution as no one there apart from the Mayor speaks any English. (Everyone everywhere else speaks some English, whatever they tell you. My French, which I always try, is so bad that as soon as they hear it they reply in English. Of course, I'm in French mode and can't switch . . .) But I had my communication all written out: 'Je suis Nigel Cox, je voudrais . . .' The counter-jumper sends me to wait by the coffee machine. Employees buy drinks from this machine every moment or two; they all talk to it. France is a highly automated country: at the station you can buy your train ticket, or something to eat, or drink, or sweets, from similar machines; or reserve a sleeper for Paris, or buy an airline ticket for anywhere in Europe, or have 50 business cards printed, or make photocopies, or do your banking—all without having to deal with a person you will have to be civil to. On the motorway the toll machine sorts

The Colour of Distance

the coins you toss into its wire basket and instantly returns you the correct change. The machines have personality: my train ticket automaton often says to me, 'Je suis hors service.' The telephone directory comes via a little TV called a Mini-Tel, which I can't work very well, despite the English language instructions. It can deliver just about anything, horoscopes, stock-market reports, the contents of department stores, flight information, but I keep getting a list of French provinces, which one do you desire? Other people play sex games on them—a guy down the road ran up a $20,000 phone bill.

M. Kettela (still at his desk most days at 6.30) waves me into his office, reads my communication, rings Works without having to look up the number. None of this, 'It's late, they'll be closed,' or, 'It's not my department,' which of course it isn't. One further call, he's got the right man. 'Ah—merci bien.' Then he explains all, very fast so I haven't got a clue what he's saying. But I can guess from his face: they're checking it out, I'm to come back in twenty minutes. 'D'accord,' I say, 'd'accord. A bientôt.' See, fluent.

The 'old town' of Menton is twelfth-century and very beautiful: long cool dark streets, high sided, like slots, wind up towards the flying bell tower of the campanile. Up, up, that's where you look, to the pale scrollwork and the frescoes fading back into the sand-coloured façades, but down, down, that's where the drinks are, so I head down to the pedestrian precinct where you are reminded that 'café' is a French word. I have calculated that if everyone in this town wanted a restaurant seat at the same time it wouldn't be a problem. These restaurant-cafés are what the French do best. The service is casual, off-hand but deceptively attentive, and of course the offerings are so wonderfully tasty. I have a bière while many people all better dressed and looking than I am stroll past in what seems to me to be terrific style. I could watch the people here forever—and they wouldn't care . . .

Upon my return M. Kettela seems to have done the trick. He talks absolutely flat out and he's probably high IQ too, I can hardly catch a thing. But I gather from his manner that he's finished with me, and I've made out 'demain', tomorrow, and he looks pleased with himself, so I go home.

Nigel Cox   191

Next morning when I arrive at 7.58am (still there, Mr McLauchlan?) I see everything's been dealt to. The earth is open, the vine has been ripped out and is lying like a length of old twine. Within my little kingdom, water is again flowing as it should (remember 'Clochemerle', remember Pagnol) and I am content. At 8.30 the foreman turns up, we shake hands, we peer at the earth and nod seriously, stroking our chins. Two other officials turn up to make sure that all impediments to the writing of fiction have been removed.

Which they have. It wasn't a big job, but all of it was done after-hours, very swiftly, for a foreigner who doesn't speak French. I hope we could match this performance at home . . .

A bientôt, New Zealand.

Menton, late April 1991

Peter Bland

Known as an actor as well as a poet, Peter Bland (born in Yorkshire, 1934) has spent roughly half his life in England, the other half in New Zealand. During the 1950s, soon after his arrival in New Zealand, Bland was associated with James K. Baxter, Louis Johnson and the 'Wellington Group'. His elegy for Johnson, 'A Last Note from Menton' (1988), won an Arvon Award in England and has been much anthologised.

A Last Note from Menton

i.m. Louis Johnson (1924–1988)

'Displacement,' you wrote, 'is a kind
of freedom . . . Let's count ourselves lucky
we *don't* belong!' Some mention then
of how Lawrence died
in sunny Vence, with freezing legs;
while back in New Mexico his allotment bloomed
with English beans. You enjoyed a sense
of ironies on the move. They
scissored at the truth. 'In the end,'
you said, 'it's always a passing love.'

Back home, you feared we were 'digging in' . . .
that old Kiwi regressive thing
disguised as growing roots. You
fought all your life for a local voice
but knew—to misquote—that it often grew
'out of the mouths of foreign Mums'.

Again and again you mention Mansfield's
'broad light of day'—that glare
she turned away from when
it pinned her to this land. That view
has still to be faced, across

tin roofs and tidal mud. Is it
a place where only prophets thrive,
never coming down from the hills
to do the washing up? You
turned away from those cold heights
to look an exile in the eye,
living the question Katherine asked:
can one stay and keep an open heart,
discard the sackcloth, let the spirit dance?

Today I almost gave myself over
to your 'friendly enemy' Colin McCahon.
Well, what's a little puritan thunder
when it gives you the shape
and feel of the land? But you'd
have none of him. In Mansfield's study
a print of *The Virgin as a Jug of Water*
and the Infant Jesus compared to a Lamp
made you hopping mad. 'It's
Kiwi Kindergarten stuff . . . Mum
knows best . . . the bullying voice of God!'
You slammed the door and drove to Cannes
hungry for Matisse, writing back
that 'life's too short to be preached at! Oh
these golden nudes with tits like melons
and flowers growing out of their bums!'
A kid's vernacular, poking its tongue
at stern big Daddy and know-all Mum.

We never finished our last chat
about Ashbery, that New York voice
always refusing to bore us with
'old anecdotes'. Unfair, I know,
but I had to laugh at your sudden roar
of bewilderment when his language shifts
from 'the merely provisional'
to the fashionably chic. In Lambland, I guess,
we're inclined to take our egos home
bruised but intact, slapping them down

like raw steak on the page. It's as if
we *need* something seen-and-known,
even roundly human, from which to face
the local bully on his own home-ground.

Which brings us to the question of place . . .
not always the same as feeling
we belong. 'We'll take *that*
from anywhere we can get it;
a kiss or the rim of a glass!'
You shunned a tribal embrace, that sense
of a race apart. What
mattered wasn't raising flags
but keeping love afloat. You liked
a busy harbour, boats bustling in
from London, New York, Camelot.

I think of you in a room not a landscape,
at home among 'domestic gifts'—
wife, children, friends, twin terrapins,
and that happy exile, your Australian cat
(always one up on the local mice).
A world within arm's reach . . .
the antithesis of that childhood house
with its '30s furniture rigidly arranged
like 'a row of cold old ladies
eaten by life and work'. That place
haunted you all your life, and made
a religion for you out of hospitality:
as if your own love could erase the pain
of a prim parental parlour
reserved for guests who never arrived.
I sensed your hatred for illusions of grandeur,
your distrust of 'the new men with no qualities'
who push the vernacular aside. 'The beach
at the end of the world,' was how
you described a life-long sense
of being born marooned. What
earthed you was your love of light. (Those

huge horizons beached outside.) Each
day arrived like a guest at your door . . .

You died where you felt alive . . . in 'old Europe',
that charnel-house of human love
where you cut through the crap of class and privilege
with such an equalising laugh. Blair
Peach died there, his skull caved in
by a bunch of *Specials* as he tried to stop
some Fascist bully-boys from playing god.
Increasingly I'm talking to the dead . . .
Jim, Renato, Stefan, yourself;
post-war émigrés and local bit-players
who belted it out, taking their bows
with more than a dash of self-conscious sweat.

Detail . . . detail . . . garlic and lemons
in a blue bowl, the moon near full,
your poems spilt like milk on the table,
the cat in the sand-box, poised like a sphinx.
I describe these things
'as they are', as you'd find them
if you were sitting here, looking out
at Rangitoto—a tent under starlight—
with a Russian cruise-ship looming by
like that moment in Fellini's *Roma*
when the little boy looks up to find
a skyscraper silently sailing past.
Our generation's almost gone:
a handful of hermits and refugees
who loosened local speech, but rarely
shaped the language with a conscious grace.
You wrote that you 'couldn't will our history
to hide behind a settler's fence'.
What a relief! All that anxious ancestry
now left to others. Your poems adrift
like paper boats or messages in bottles,
careless of landfall, happy to be themselves.

Janet Frame

Janet Frame (1924–2004) was one of New Zealand's most significant writers. She published 11 novels, numerous collections of stories, a book of verse and an acclaimed autobiography. In 1974 Frame was Katherine Mansfield Memorial Fellow, during which time she wrote a letter (in French) to the *Nice Matin* complaining about the noise of helicopters over the Mansfield Room. (This letter, she would later relate gleefully, was the extent of her published works originally written in French.) Following the appearance of her three-volume autobiography and Jane Campion's film *An Angel at My Table*, Janet Frame now has a considerable reputation in France, and many of her books have been published in French translation. Her 1979 novel *Living in the Maniototo* includes a flashback to her time in Menton, where, in typical Frame fashion, she transforms the Mansfield Room into the Margaret Rose Hurndell Memorial Room.

from Living in the Maniototo

And I thought of the room in Menton in the villa where Margaret Rose Hurndell had lived, and how I had visited the room. I walked up a narrow street beneath a railway bridge and up another street that had once been a Roman Road, and on the left I saw the plaque, *Margaret Rose Hurndell Memorial Room*, giving the date of her birth and death (born 1930—the same year as Princess Margaret Rose—died in 1957; and like Peter Wallstead largely unknown until after her death) and a list of her writings. The garden was overgrown with weeds, the stairs leading to the small garden were thick with sodden leaves and fragments of paper thrown off the street. I put the Margaret Rose Hurndell Key (which I had borrowed) in the lock and pushed open the sun-blistered wooden door which permitted itself to open halfway: it had 'dropped' like an old used womb. I walked in. I opened the tiny windows, pushing back the branches that crowded against them. The room slowly became 'aired' like old stored linen. Small chutchutting birds with whistlings and secretive noises began stirring outside. A cool wind blew through the windows and out the

197

door, a between-winter-and-spring wind. There was an air of desolation in the room and beyond it. A water-spotted plaque inside gave further details of Margaret Rose Hurndell's career. There were a few straight-backed vicarage-type chairs in the room, and a desk and a bookshelf (an Armstrong Fellow came each year to work in the memorial room); and layers of cold along the bare, tiled floor. I could hear the grass swaying in the neglected garden, and the brittle rustling of the flax bush, now a mass of soaring green spears, which a sympathetic writer had planted near the crumbling wall.

Here, I thought, if one were a spirit or dead, is a sanctuary. With a sudden rush of wind, dead leaves, twigs and a scrap of paper blew inside. The air of desolation and neglect increased: the chill, of the wind and of the spirit, intensified and there was the kind of peace that one feels walking among the dead and listening, as the dead may, at a great distance from the world and its movement and noise.

I went to explore the small garden and found a green garden seat which I cleared, brushing away the bruised ripe loquats fallen everywhere from the huge loquat tree; and I lay down, half in sun, half in shadow, looking up at the lemon tree in the neighboring garden of the Villa Florita. I closed my eyes. The sun came out again, moving quickly, and was on my face, burning. I changed my position on the seat. The sun was once again hidden behind cloud, the air was chill again, the flax rustled with a brittle snapping sound and the secretive small birds once again began their whispering and chittering. I fell asleep. And when I woke I shivered with cold. The mountains were harsh and grey with fallen used daylight, softened in the crevices with the blue of distance and evening.

So that was the Rose Hurndell Room! I dreamed of it, and of my own home in Bannockburn Road, Blenheim, and the two lives I had known there, and the daily use which marriage makes, one of the other, as the light makes of the twin slopes of the mountain, and I was glad that the colour of distance was beginning to touch my view of my life in Bannockburn Road.

Michael Harlow

A practising Jungian psychotherapist, Michael Harlow has published seven collections of poetry. Born in the United States in 1937, he travelled extensively before settling in New Zealand in 1968. He was holder of the Katherine Mansfield Memorial Fellowship 1986, during which time he wrote the poems which follow. These first appeared in his 1992 collection, *Giotto's Elephant*.

How Nice

In this story you are walking down a wide avenue
Park or Fifth or the Champs-Elysées and suddenly
Without even the traffic lights changing from
Red to green you see all these women pushing blue
Prams with pennants flying and you think, 'How
Nice'—at least one half of the world is out
On parade and besides spring has just entered the
City but when you look into the prams you see what
You have been hearing for the very first time: you
See that all the babies are radios playing jazz . . .

Paschal Numbers

At Passover week
The first full sun
In a fortnight of rain
He began to discover
The garden and the birds
In the garden and the gold
Carp rising the green water

On the Venetian sundial
He began to trace the time
Turning in a circle of light

He said, measuring his words
'Now, I will tell everyone
The story of numbers,'
And he did that, spooning them
Out of the air with his quick
Hands—he could see
We were in urgent need
Of information.

Clos du Peyronnet

Stephanie de Montalk

Wellington-based, Stephanie de Montalk (born 1945) is the author of three collections of poetry and a remarkable account of her second cousin, Count Geoffrey Potocki de Montalk, *Unquiet World* (2001). As well as evoking the life and times of the 'poet, polemicist, pagan, pretender to the throne of Poland—and one of the great eccentrics of the twentieth century', the book follows the younger de Montalk on numerous visits to the poet's dwelling outside Draguignan, between Nice and Marseilles.

from Unquiet World

I first met Potocki in the summer of 1968. John and I were travelling and camping in Europe, and as we planned to be passing through the French Riviera, only a short drive from the town in Provence where he had been living since leaving London in the late 1940s, I had made arrangements to meet him.

I had written from Scotland before we left. My father, who was his first cousin, had been receiving his hand-printed poems for the Feast of Saturn each Christmas for some years, and knew where he could be found: the Villa Vigoni, Chemin de St Martin, Draguignan. Potocki had replied immediately, without preamble, and in a style which would become familiar:

> Dear Stéphanie,
> What do you mean, I have probably never heard of you?
> I printed your name in the BLOOD ROYAL referred to in the enclosed pamphlet . . .
> It is nice your having heard of 'my activities in London in the l930s' but what was much more important was my activities during the war. My so far unpublished book about it is called My Private War Against England. You doubtless know that I claimed the Polish Throne, but I wonder if you know that I was the only person with the guts to publish the truth about the Katyn massacre in English during the war

(naturally the English government knew perfectly well that this massacre was committed by their criminal allies, the Soviets).

Also, I broke the English censorship of the Polish papers in England, by the simple method of asking the Polish politicians what was in the censored spaces, whereupon I printed the gist of it in English without asking the permission of the censor's office. This enabled the Poles to take each matter up with the English, and ask: Why is this British-born Count Potocki allowed to print this, if we aren't? Naturally the English couldn't say to the Poles: 'Well, we can't do anything with Potocki. He doesn't ask our permission.'

Details of my great-grandmother's descent from Alexander, Earl of Dunfermline, followed. They were of some interest because at the time I was nursing the Earl of Elgin, and John and I were living in on his sixteenth-century estate only a few kilometres from Dunfermline. He went on:

> I can probably put you and your husband up, that is if the new room is finished, which it probably will be. How will you be arriving? Are you driving a car? You should try to arrange in full detail for me to meet you in Draguignan, for though this place is only two miles from the town, it is difficult to find the first time. Otherwise I had better send you very full sailing directions as to how to get here. How well do you speak French?
>
> You are descended as my book shows, from the most famous generations of Chiefs of most of the great Scots clans, but not Bruce, the Chief being the Earl of Elgin & Kincardine. But I haven't yet done the Sutherland side of the pedigree, and Bruce may be there for all I know.
> Best wishes to your husband. I hope he is a Scot at least? Your affectionate cousin, Potocki of Montalk.

My knowledge of my cousin was limited. For as long as I could remember, the de Montalk family in New Zealand had dismissed him as an embarrassment. He had left his wife and small daughter unsupported in order to 'follow the golden road to Samarkand', to live abroad, to be a poet. He was 'eccentric'—the word was usually delivered in a disparaging tone; a 'pagan'—the tone faltered here as if at the edge of evil; someone who worshipped Apollo and sunbathed naked. He was a man who wore sandals and robes, and grew his hair; a 'madman' who claimed the throne of Poland. And together with his brother Cedric, who had also left New Zealand and remained abroad, he used the family name in full, retained the title of count, and not only acknowledged his aristocratic Polish ancestry but flaunted it. One didn't do such things. If it was good enough for Count Joseph Wladislas Edmond Potocki de Montalk to dispense with his title and diminish his surname to de Montalk on arrival in New Zealand from France in 1868, it was appropriate his antipodean descendants did likewise. Moreover, Potocki's obscenity trial in London in 1932, his subsequent imprisonment, his pro-German stance during the war—my father, who had fought in Greece and North Africa, regarded him as a traitor—and his ongoing appearances in the British courts and press, had impugned the family name and the wider family wanted nothing to do with him.

But I was of another generation. At college I'd been secretly delighted by the sporadic, albeit disparaging, reports about him in the New Zealand papers—photographs had shown him to be a handsome and provocative man—and I'd been amused and even flattered when my mother, frustrated by my teenage rebellions, had exclaimed: 'You're just like the Count!' Later, I'd observed that with his long hair, sandals and robes he was likely to be a man ahead of his time. And, intrigued by his trial, I'd taken the trouble to read about it. In fact, I'd discovered sympathetic discussion of both the facts of the case and the six-month prison sentence in Alec Craig's *The Banned Books of England*, which I'd obtained from the public library and read on a day off from the hospital while sunbathing on a Wellington beach. I'd decided that a relative responsible for an event described by Craig as 'a sensational obscenity case', and the recipient of a sentence that W. B. Yeats spoke of as 'criminally brutal', certainly merited further investigation.

. . .

Draguignan is a large market-town inland between Nice and Marseille, in the administrative region of Var, a *département* of forests, vineyards—some of the oldest in France—and immense blue skies. In summer the air in the Var is thick with cicadas, wild herbs and resinous trees; the landscape shimmers. In winter, when the mistral blows down from the north for days, even weeks at a time, the hearths of the stone cottages come into their own; I have heard it said that writers like the mistral—its powerful bite, its persistence, its strong poetic force. Built on the site of a former Roman military post in the fifth century AD, Draguignan was named after a dragon which lived in the marshlands and was said to have terrorised the townsfolk. As the crow flies, the town is only around twenty kilometres from the coast, although the journey by road or rail takes over an hour.

I have no clear memories of Draguignan in the summer of 1968 beyond an impression of old stone and men sitting in squares. In the fading light of a long day it looked like any of the small towns we'd passed through *en route*. Today it is a busy commercial centre, part-modern, part-medieval, servicing sizeable wheat-, olive- and grape-growing communities and, on the outskirts of the town, near the turn-off to the St Martin district, France's largest artillery academy. There are pavement cafés on shaded boulevards, covered markets, a museum and, on a hill above the narrow streets and bent walls of the old quarter, the seventeenth-century clock tower for which the town is noted. A large number of brass plaques in the main streets suggests that Draguignan is well served by medical specialists. Last time I was in the town—after Potocki had died—a taxi driver told me the specialists like to live there because the restaurants, wine and climate are good, and it's close to the coast.

I do remember, though, that we had difficulty making ourselves understood. Although Draguignan is close to the Côte d'Azur, it is not on the tourist route, and in 1968 almost no one spoke English (I had only School Certificate French, and John the Scottish equivalent). It took for ever to locate Potocki. The Chemin de St Martin (later renamed Chemin des Faïsses) was not on our street map, and Potocki was not in the phone book. We should have made arrangements to meet him, as he suggested, but with postal services uncertain and our plans changing daily we had decided to chance it. Finally, a gendarme was able to give us some directions but, when we drove out into the countryside, there were no signposts. We spent the next two hours among sloping wooded hills making fruitless ventures in diminishing light down unmarked and unsealed roads. Eventually, our accidental wanderings led us to the town dump, where a couple pulling garden rubbish from the boot of a late-model car recognised Potocki's name, and led the way to the residence of the Controller of Lands. This was a lucky break, because the controller happened to be a personal friend of Potocki and was able to take us straight to him.

We approached the turn-off to the Villa Vigoni slowly along a thin lumpy road between low stone walls. It would have been easy to miss: for a kilometre or more the land had been overgrown with no obvious signs of habitation. However, as we pulled up behind the controller's car, just beyond a small wood, we saw that well back from the road there was a narrow, double-level dwelling, with a terracotta tiled roof, hiding in long grass. The controller, who confessed to a fear of dogs, was unwilling to approach the building on foot and so, unsure of the exact whereabouts of the driveway, we pressed on our horn and waited with him at the side of the road. After a few minutes there was a shout of welcome and a figure appeared waving and striding, and motioning to a point at which we could turn onto the property. We made our way carefully through the high grass, our Austin Minivan chewing unevenly along an uncertain track. It was difficult to know where the driveway stopped and the lower levels of the property started. If Potocki owned a vehicle it wasn't a large one. As the villa came more closely into view, we could see that it was a somewhat ramshackle stone cottage on which attempts at renovation with the aid of bottles, rocks, slabs of marble, wiring and piping—materials Potocki was later to refer to as 'deliberately chosen rubbish'—were still being made. A small car stood to one side—a Citroën Deux Chevaux, early model, bottle green with British and French identification plates. His standard—a small flag bearing the *Piława* or coat of arms of the Potocki family—hung limply from the front right-hand bumper.

We stopped the van short of the villa, where Potocki was waiting, and were greeted by a slight man wearing a red, long-sleeved, open-necked shirt which might have been silk, a pair of light-coloured riding breeches, and sandals. Although he was then sixty-five, he moved easily, with the energy of a much younger person, and there was something about his appearance that was at once elegant and compelling: the hair swept back from the forehead, perhaps, the assurance, the manner of speaking—he spoke with what would have been described at the time as an 'educated English accent'. He greeted us graciously and with warmth, shaking us by the hand, kissing me lightly on the cheek, smiling, inquiring. I was the first person from the New Zealand branch of the family, including the daughter he had abandoned when she was a child, to meet with him in more than forty years. The controller invited us all to join him for dinner, but Potocki declined. He explained that we would eat later, at the restaurant of a friend.

That evening we dined in a dimly lit stone room on a hillside on the outskirts of Draguignan. Potocki was welcomed with obvious pleasure by the female restaurateur, who seated us at a small table, brought local red wine and bread, and, after consulting with him in French, plucked a guitar solo from the record-player and replaced it with a classical track. After a while she produced a menu—the same sheet of paper she'd been taking table to table. It listed only a couple of items, entered by hand, and she waited as Potocki glanced at the page. He touched her arm. 'The food is so good, selection's simply a formality,' he said, ordering chicken. Her dark looks—she could have been Spanish—and the stone room—its roughly plastered walls, the candles—made me think of Hilaire Belloc:

Do you remember an inn,
Miranda?
Do you remember an inn?

The main course was served. I recall burnished portions of chicken topped with parsley, mushrooms and croutons, served at the table, straight from the pot in which they had simmered with onions, wine and the steam of fresh herbs. And the rhythm of 'Tarantella':

> And the tedding and the spreading
> Of the straw for a bedding,
> And the fleas that tease in the High Pyrenees,
> And the wine that tasted of the tar?

I remembered that around the time I first read this poem, as a teenager, I had first seen Potocki's photo in a newspaper in Wellington—the famous photo in which his hair falls below his shoulders and he wears a beret and cloak, and holds the black cat he called Franco.

Soon, warm with wine and rich food, he began to speak of his past. And he spoke as he had written, in twists and turns, darting from subject to subject with passion and wit and frequently with bitterness, but with little sense of exchange. He spoke of events, people and times in his life of which we had little or no knowledge, without explanation, without context. He spoke almost ceaselessly, pausing only to eat, drink and exchange smiles with his female host. John and I sat entranced. From time to time we glanced at each other and shrugged, discreetly. Did he know we were there? When dessert finally arrived we were heavy with stories of self-proclaimed genius, political and legal intrigue, personal persecution and glorious ancestry. He had given a superlative performance. Much later we were to hear the stories again, and again, frequently word for word, with the same tilt of the head, the rage and softening of the blue eyes, the preoccupation with plot and counter-plot and his own unrecognised genius. The devastating smile.

'Miranda' served sugared raspberries and cream, and coffee, and joined us for liqueurs 'on the house'. At around midnight we drove back to the villa. We crawled into our sleeping-bag with our heads spinning, the candle-yellow room going around and around

Stephanie de Montalk   207

Glancing,
Dancing,
Backing and advancing,
Snapping of the clapper to the spin
Out and in—
And the Ting, Tong, Tang of the guitar!

Who was 'Driven Mud'? What was 'Katyn'? Why was he a neglected literary figure? 'How is it possible,' we asked ourselves in whispers, 'for someone to have been so consistently wronged?'

The next day was wet. We rose early to find him already at work, pedalling the huge iron press which stood in the rough brick and stone side room he called the printery. We had declined his invitation to sleep indoors—the cottage, although double-storeyed, was cramped—and had pitched our tent on a patch of flattened grass to the side of the house. Between breakfast and lunch and for most of the afternoon he printed on the 100-year-old Marinoni platen machine. We also stayed inside, comfortable in the living room, reading, cooking on bottled gas, and looking through his files and huge library. There were thousands of books. The cottage was dark and restful, its silence broken only by the muffled sound of the rain and the creaking of his press.

The downstairs room, which also served as kitchen and spare bedroom, was cosy, homely, somewhat dusty, more a room of working clutter than outright disorder. It had a low, beamed roof and a concrete floor, and small windows which, I sensed, would on a fine day face away from the sun. The walls were covered with books, and every available surface seemed to have been given over to paper—blank printing paper, hand-corrected proofs, labels and cardboard for covers. There were a couple of shabby but soft chairs by a brick fireplace, a divan for guests, and two waist-high dressers with drawers, which served as kitchen cupboards and bench. Above the bench, to one side, a glass-fronted wall cabinet contained the pantry: tins of tea and biscuits sent by friends from abroad, cheese, eggs, smeared bottles of vinegar, red wine and olive oil. The rest of the wall was studded with hooks and nails from which saucepans and other cooking utensils hung, and woven containers holding vegetables and strings of garlic and onions, and bread. There was no plumbing, no kitchen sink, no electricity, no telephone. The lines and mains from Draguignan had not yet travelled this far. Potocki had his drinking water delivered in huge bottles of green-tinted glass, drew his household water from a hand-pump well halfway between the cottage and the road, and washed his dishes in a plastic basin on the dresser bench. He cooked with bottled gas, lit the room with a paraffin lamp, and showered outside in the summer, in water still sun-warm from the hose he had somehow connected to the well.

On our arrival he had taken us on a tour of the villa, and we had inspected his arrangements with interest. Adjacent to the living room was the printery, The Mélissa Press. It was poorly lit, the stonework was rough and the floorboards incomplete. Clearly, it would be cold during winter. Above the living room, with access by a steep and narrow set of wooden stairs, was his bedroom, which also served as a study. This room too was low-roofed and the chief impression was of a haphazard preoccupation with paper. The walls were lined with files and books—a quick glance suggested hundreds of volumes of poetry, dictionaries in dozens of languages, antiquarian publications, classical works, genealogical and astrological texts. (I don't remember any individual titles, but a subsequent visit by John Macalister, whose article 'Count Potocki of Montalk, a private library in Provence', appeared in *The Private Library* in 1984, revealed that, among the modern poets in a collection of more than 700 books of poetry, Yeats, Roy Campbell and Edgell Rickword were 'well-represented'; that the 'pornography shelf' held *Lady Chatterley's Lover*, *Lolita*, *The Kama Sutra* and *The Perfumed Garden*—titles 'unexciting by today's standards'; and that the library was 'low on novels, perhaps to be expected from one whose idea of true literature is poetry'.) There was also a well-blanketed double bed, with a polished wooden headboard on which the Potocki coat of arms had been skilfully carved and painted, and, at the foot of the bed, an upright piano. Alongside the door to the garden, Potocki had pushed back a curtain to reveal a niche in which he had set up a small table as the altar at which he worshipped the god of the sun. Then he had opened the bedroom door onto concrete steps leading to the unshaded upper level of the property optimistically spoken of as the back garden. 'Winston Churchill's down there,' he said, indicating a steep set of steps to a shelter below and to the side of the cottage. 'You'll have to excuse him—he's a bucket.'

At some point during the day he ran short of paper, so we drove him into Draguignan to replenish his supply, and buy steak for the evening meal. On the way home we stopped off at his other properties: an overgrown holding in the suburb of Flayosc, and 2000 square metres of olive grove in the Vallon de Gandi, close to the villa. There was a small building, previously an olive harvester's hut, in the valley, and we clambered about in the wet grass inspecting the dark derelict rooms in which he had first lived after leaving England. We learnt that he also owned land in Dorset, England.

That evening over dinner, the tales of heredity and history resumed. We sat around the table tantalised by more tales of injustice, half told, never explained. As previously, we were reluctant to appear uninformed, to intrude upon the performance. Contrary to Cedric's concern, there was no untoward mention of sex. We lingered with him until well into the evening. The lamp softened the room and deepened the red wine in our glasses. Time and place seemed slightly unreal. I could see us all as if from a distance, laughing and talking in a small circle of light in the dark countryside. In the midst of a revolution in France, here we were meeting with a true revolutionary. 'He gives me hope for older age,' John said later.

Catherine Chidgey

Catherine Chidgey (born 1970) held the Meridian Energy Katherine Mansfield Memorial Fellowship in 2001, during which time she worked on her third novel, *The Transformation*. Tampa, Florida, 1898 is the book's setting; however, in this extract, the main character—a wig-maker by the name of Monsieur Lucien Goulet III—reminisces about a profitable visit to Gorbio, a hillside village near Menton and favoured walking destination of Katherine Mansfield fellows.

from The Transformation

'Have you ever visited France, Monsieur Flood?' I asked, although I was well aware that he never travels beyond the swamps.

'France?'

'I am thinking of a region in Provence, where the snail is especially esteemed.'

'Go on,' he said.

'Four men go into the fields,' I said. 'The first carries a drum, which he beats to simulate thunder. The second carries a watering can with which he sprinkles the ground in imitation of rain. The third carries a veiled lamp which he uncovers for a second or two at a time—'

'The lightning!' said Flood, as over-excited as a backwoods Revivalist.

'The lightning. And the fourth man—he collects the snails, who love wet weather, as you know, and who have been fooled into believing that a storm has broken.'

'Intriguing,' said Flood.

I paused. 'To answer your question, Monsieur, the reason for the cost is that the hair comes from so far away. With such a fine, dark sheen as yours to match, I must look to the Continent, and in fact to this very region of France, for my material.'

And I told him of the misty cliffside village of Gorbio, which is indeed in Provence, although shortly before I visited it in the 1860s it was part of Italy. I did not bother to explain this to the thinning Mr Flood, for history lessons do not sell hair-pieces.

'In Gorbio, on the day of Corpus Christi, the Procession des Limaces is celebrated,' I said, and I saw my listener frown at the foreign expression. 'The Procession of Slugs,' I said, 'although in the Provençal dialect it is understood as snails.' The magic word; he beamed. 'Snail shells are filled with olive oil and wicks, and placed in every window, and when it is dark they are struck with a taper, and the people begin to follow the trail of little flames.'

I described for him the White Penitents, an order of flagellants who lead the procession dressed in snowy robes, and I described the girls who lean from the windows, their dark curtains of hair burnished by the flames. And as I spoke, my voice ushering him through the coiling streets, the White Penitents just ahead of us like spirits, the shells shimmering with oil, I felt such a stillness descend on me that I wanted to stay in that misty village, that place of shifting boundaries. Privately I recalled how I once had found myself in Gorbio on the night of the procession without a place to stay. It was my practice to arrange lodgings in the house or barn of one of the women who sold me her hair, but that day it seemed that all the females of Gorbio visited me in the village square, and I was so busy that I had not stopped to organise shelter of any kind. Most chattered about the procession, and it crossed my mind that perhaps they were ridding themselves of their hair as an acknowledgement to the White Penitents, who not only shaved their heads but whipped themselves and willingly performed the deeds despised or feared by others: the visiting of the dying, the burial of victims of infectious disease. I joined the procession, certain I would meet one of my donors who would oblige me with accommodation. Perhaps it was a trick of the light or the mist, but as we made our way along the close streets every face seemed distorted by the oily flames and I recognised nobody. I was just beginning to consider sleeping on one of the olive terraces—although they make a hard bed, I had done so before—when I was greeted by a pretty girl who watched from her window.

'You are Monsieur Dubois, the hair merchant?' she called.

'I am he.'

She bent forward, her dark hair billowing like a cloak, and if I had lifted my hands I might have touched it. 'How much?' she said.

'I would have to examine it more closely.'

She moved from the window, setting the flames trembling in their shells, and in a moment she was at the door and inviting me inside and pouring me a tumbler of wine.

I lifted her hair in my hands, as I had done with countless other females in village squares and fairgrounds. Here, however, where the ceiling was low and the walls were creeping with roses—surely a fresco, although they looked real—the action acquired an intimacy for which I was not prepared. Her neck glimmered in the light of the oil-filled shells and the candles in their bronze sconces.

'Why didn't you come to the square today, when I was cutting the other girls' hair?' I said.

'I don't know,' she said. 'Maybe I was frightened.' She sipped at her wine, the tendon at the side of her neck flexing and relaxing.

My fingers had crept to her collarbone now, and to the hollow at the base of her throat. I could feel her pulse.

'I can't cut at night,' I said. 'We'll have to wait until morning.'

She nodded, pouring me some more wine. 'Do you have anywhere to sleep?'

'No,' I said.

'Then you'll stay with me.' She blew out the candles, but left the snail shells to gutter out one by one.

Under the musty sheets she began to kiss my face and chest, her little tongue leaving trails on my skin. 'Do you have to leave tomorrow?' she said. 'Can't you stay longer?'

In a voice unlike my own I said that perhaps I could, and I felt I was in neither Italy nor France but some borderless land.

It may have been the wine, to which I was unaccustomed in those days, but I had never slept so soundly, nor have I since.

Catherine Chidgey

When I awoke the room was just becoming light, and on the walls the painted roses wound about their painted lattice. My young companion lay face down, and as I lifted the covers I saw that she had coiled herself into a knot, her limbs and back and head a tawny whorl against the linen. I hesitated for a moment, then unsheathed my scissors and began to cut. She did not wake, but obligingly stirred her head so that I could reach the other side, and it was then that I saw she was not a girl at all but a woman of forty or more: twice my age. Perhaps it was for this reason that I pulled some coins from my purse and placed them on the pillow, shiny little second thoughts. They amounted to much more than I would have paid had she come to me in the square, but by now I was anxious to leave. And so I slipped outside, to where the streets were cool and silent, and charred shells lined the window ledges, marking my way toward the next village. As I hurried up the mountain to Sainte-Agnès, Gorbio faded below me, and when it had disappeared into the mist I sat and caught my breath. There was not enough air up there. All around me grew patches of mandrake, and clusters of starry cranesbill, and sometimes little moths of the same shade of blue flew up from the leaves, and I had to look very closely to tell the flower from the insect. I held the skein of dark hair in my lap and wondered whether I might not keep it for myself, tucked away in a place where my master would never look. But I could think of no such place.

'A celebration of the snail,' George Flood was saying. 'An homage to the mollusc.'

I could not help but marvel that the home of this drool of a man is each week visited by Marion Unger. Before he could expand any further, I flung open the door to Bluebeard's Chamber and began unhooking lengths of hair. My stock is plentiful since I have taken on my Cuban, who has a nose for the job and sometimes collects more hair in one night than I did in a week.

'Shall we match your colour?' I said, and I was back in Tampa.

Michael Gifkins

After his time as Katherine Mansfield Memorial Fellow in 1985, Michael Gifkins (born 1945) published a number of short stories set on the Riviera. These were included in two subsequent collections: *Summer is the Côte d'Azur* (1987) and *The Amphibians* (1989). In recent years Michael Gifkins has devoted his energies to his work as a literary agent.

Dedication

You wake each morning bride to the day. A gossamer invitation, your nightgown sheens your body's hidden line. You pause before the mirror. You smile. You toss back glistening curls. Outside, light fingers damp tufts of mimosa, creeps in across the sill. Light in great lakes exerts its calm upon the sea. Along the Croisette, a general walks his dog. The general is stiff with great campaigns.

You dress your body. You are still smiling. At each fresh wave of memory the dog quivers, strains forward upon the leash at signposts from dogs before him. They stretch as far as the eye can see.

You are entering the Carlton, ice-cream cake of a grand hotel. It is night. All afternoon the people have waited for this moment. You imagine it is you they want to see. You are wearing your little black dress. Gendarmes with submachine guns line the steps. There are ropes to hold back the crowds. You clutch your ticket tighter still.

Offshore, the great white sharks gnaw lazily at their moorings. The moon beats a path to your empty room. Terrorists in velvet staterooms recite the Koran, fiddling with unsourced weaponry, declining offers of drinks. In a bath that seethes with Chanel a toe stabs at a gilded tap.

Up the stairs you go, unfazed by the crowds. Your escort is not handsome; you are a small group, from a country far away. You laugh, catching the attention of the *paparazzi*. You press yourself against him.

It is like being in a revolution. Outside the crowd is calling for the star of the festival, who is also your countryman and the reason you are here. They distort his name so that you believe they are chanting for an American car. When he returns he seems younger than a schoolboy. Women twice his age are trying to catch his eye. Fame makes his girlfriend distant from him by more than the twenty thousand kilometres he has journeyed. He prods gloomily at his *escargots*.

You are seated on the right hand of the festival director. You reply in a tongue that is not your own. Waiters bowl round like hooped snakes, pausing occasionally to hiss obscenities in your ear. The director toys with bread like a child, teasing it out into shreds.

You would like to help him, tell him that art is long and life has a habit of being short. But he is replaying his much-publicised argument with the internationally acclaimed actor . . . words were shouted in four languages in the lobby of the hotel. The actor publicly denounced the festival, left his honour behind him like a bad smell. It is said openly now, what they only dared whisper before.

The actor's face is the mask of death.

I am here on business, in the perennial search for funds. You hear of this eventually, though it is not the reason that we meet. This is at one of the many cocktail parties, where the champagne goes on and on. You glow from inside, like the Church of St-Michel; your eyes transmit a wonder which up close becomes a laugh. *Oh where do you go to, my lovely . . . ?* the old tune asks.

'I'm from New Zealand,' you announce when we are finally introduced. The way you say it is both challenge and apology, why I can't be sure. Only later do I tell you that I know your country well from books.

We dance all night with your friends and then promenade to greet the dawn. I escort you back to your small hotel. In a side-street *tabac* we have coffee; there are glistening bikes parked outside. The black T-shirts and red scarves of their riders are your adrenalin to start the day.

'I can say,' you remember, 'that I was kissed by a handsome man at dawn.'

We are walking under palm trees and night scents hang heavy in the air. I take a spray of jasmine and twine it through your hair. You are damp on your skin from dancing, and cold now to the touch. I kiss you as I might kiss a sister, not someone recently met.

Today I meet my backers, in a walled garden in Cap Martin—it is as familiar to me as loving, this slow seduction of money from its vaults. On impulse I suggest your presence. I hold my hands upturned, in supplication, above their wondrous marble table with its exotic food and drink. (This is a gesture I have learned from someone else.) They are a cagey pair, the banker and his mistress, indulging some private fantasy that I must endorse without further question.

'But she is so *spectacular*!' Mme de Ferrier refers to you as though you were not there. 'And to think, all this way from New Zealand! *La Mansfield* would necessarily have been quite, quite jealous.' One day she will phone me transatlantic to discuss the character of Virginia Woolf.

I acquiesce with suitable deference to their quite unreasonable demands. They discuss their favourite stories, speaking as the characters would themselves. It is early evening when they ask the manservant to bring a pen.

You feel tired now; you are starting to wilt. You are pleased with the way things are.

The agreement is signed over cognac, so old that Fritz could well be serving ghosts. We are gathered like a family in the lengthening shadow of the land-based wall. '*They would never be alone together again,*' Mme de Ferrier proposes the toast that binds us all.

I suggest we go to the Casino but our host declines; the prospect of money in his hands has lost its power to amuse him. He warns us—without irony, I think—of the extent to which commerce can be inimical to art. You ask that I take you to the villa where Katherine Mansfield tried to arrest her slow decline. You feel in your bones that I need all the assistance you can give.

It is a small building, quite unspectacular compared with some of the finer residences in Garavan. Upstairs there is darkness, but a dim light burns in the ground floor room which is now a memorial to the writer. It is a poet from New Zealand, on the fellowship which bears the writer's name. You are embarrassed. Quite irrationally (because you know her), you suddenly change your mind. You wait nervously as I try to frame the villa for the film. There is no way I can make of it any more than it is.

You turn to me and hold me fiercely, pressing me to your chest. Your feeling is that you are awkward, heroic. We stand like this for a long moment and you ask me how it will end. You have no idea of my patience. You quiver with light and clangour. Your world is suddenly awry. It is the express from Ventimiglia, bursting through the cushion of the night.

You are motoring through the region of the Loire to your assignation in the south. The small Citroën you pick up the day before from the tourist scheme in the Champs de Mars. You are protected by Autostop: a newer car should this new car break down; accommodation, transport, insurance. They try to sell you extras which they present with Gallic flair—wheel kits, foglights, everything that *les madames* would want to cause their journey to be more *confortable*. You do not say anything. You are driven, both of you giggling, to the bowels of a huge parking building in a district you do not understand. For your benefit and your education the chauffeur takes unnecessary risks. There is your little car. A mechanic tells you what to do in all of fifteen seconds. You emerge into rush-hour traffic. You stop, you start. You try to remember your left side from your right. You are behind a big *camion*. It seems that all Paris is burning. Your car is filled with smoke. It is an early summer. You phone Autostop.

'It is regrettable.'

They have neglected to put the oil in the car.

The second car is dark red, the colour of your blood. Parked outside this smallest chateau, it reminds you now of London. It is the off-season. You make an appointment with the concierge by phone. He gets up. He dresses. He breakfasts.

The Colour of Distance

He takes his time. You press every bell at every entrance to the castle.

Eventually it emerges from a high gothic window, this severely correct French student head. He recalls for you a Truffaut movie, along with everything else in France. *Dix minutes.* Deer as a courtly sideline graze the boundary fence. You inspect the crypt while you wait. You suddenly feel cold. Maxine is asking you about AIDS. She thinks you are far more likely to get it from blood, in spite of precautions. She carries twelve dozen of her own precautions and you comment on her dedicated optimism. She is your best friend, having recently lost her father. In your purse are the three Durex you keep as a talisman; it would be foolish, coming this far, to undergo a merely topical demise.

Inside the chateau is history, fast forward with no concessions. In whispers you translate. You are a party of tourists. There are two of you. There can be no deviation from history as it is laid down. It takes forty minutes, twenty lifetimes. You tip the student twenty francs.

At the crossroads back from the chateau there is a typical country café. The owners seem retarded and you notice tinned peas upon a shelf. You ask for espresso, anything. There are small vacuum flasks on the counter. To your consternation these contain the coffee. They pour you lukewarm cups of tar.

Maxine does the driving; she says she feels it is her duty and you do not have the energy to object. On the autoroute you colonise the slow lane as fuel-injected Europe slips past at 200 kilometres an hour. 'Better to travel safely than to arrive dead on time.' Your best friend winces as you laugh.

Your son has difficulty walking. It is a mild condition which may in later life provide the basis for reflection upon the norm. Your daughter, on the other hand, is quite healthy. Recently she has acquired the habit of rubbing her body slowly against your startled male friends. You could, if you wish, read whole novels in their eyes. You do not want to warn her.

A friend of your ex-lover's phones to tell you that he (your lover) collects only exceptional women. (She imagines this will please you.) Currently there is an involvement with an archaeologist, which explains why he did not meet your plane. The archaeologist is a young Frenchwoman of great vivacity and piercing intelligence who is making her contribution to a post-modern understanding of Pharaonic ritual. You picture them both quite easily beneath a nightmare weight of stone. You are pleased for your ex-lover, that he is sharing the passion which leads her to the burial chamber. His own special project is an exploration of the infrastructure of the aesthetic impulse of what remains of the Western world. You consider this as you spend the whole day in a London hospital. You are fascinated by the soft bubbling of your own and another's blood.

The coffee is so bitter that you need to cleanse yourself with wine.

We are walking the seacoast from Monaco in the direction of Cap Martin. A drugged-out Princess Stéphanie enters an exclusive private hospital. Her press release claims stress caused through overworking. A famous actress leaves the road at 140 kilometres an hour. Each day twenty kilograms of letters bear her the country's undying affection. Distinguished surgeons contemplate the reconstruction of the muscles of her face. On front pages her Porsche lies crumpled. The advertisement beside it is for Veuve Clicquot champagne.

You imagine that our picnic will make you homesick. When I ask you why, you cannot say.

We are jammed amongst the rocks which tumble on the seafront of the great estates. Through the tropical profusion of walled gardens their towers are glimpsed against the sky. A fisherman (you call him *piscator*) is busy down beneath us. The weather is unseasonal, but he is dressed in suit and tie. You say that it is the ghost of Italo Calvino.

The ants are feasting on crumbs of *pain complet*. You demand that I pass my glass. It was the horror of her own insignificance, you claim, that caused Katherine Mansfield's death. You wave your hand about you, encompassing the scene. The fisherman, I mention, might be delighted to see you bathe.

Your son was born with a massive tumour; it was pressing

on his brain. Though the terminology surprised you, the experts pronounced it to be benign. You watched as he emerged from that first operation, a tiny parcel swaddled like a corpse. Every year as he grew bigger, they replaced the device inside his head.

I disagree with you about Mansfield; we discuss the psychopathology of health. Your son slept in a cot beside you, so you could feed him in the night. Pursing tiny lips, he would take your warm and heavy breast. You talked to him as he suckled, asking him if he was ready yet to swap. You smile fondly at this memory; his first words were 'other side!'

Each evening I review my plans; the shape of the film to come. There will be love interest, though my treatment of Murry is bound to attract comment. Perhaps the purists would prefer him cast in a traditionally demeaning role? There will be the self-confidence of a major talent abroad, sustained by backward glances at a sun-filled antipodean childhood; there will be the recognition of the pain of loss, the intimations of mortality. But above all, there will be the gathering dark.

You move your face above me, as if to shield me from the glare. I blink to adjust my vision to the sudden change of light. The cascade of curls frames the perfect oval of your face. The sheen of your teeth is like a string of pearls.

When we awake, both sun and fisherman are gone. You feel that perhaps your mood should change. In a small café you drink glass after glass of pernod, watch the water cloud the clear spirit. You intimidate the waiter with an *hauteur* I had not imagined before, calling for olives, for a clean glass. You organise where we should dine. You even comment on the style of my shirt.

Your head is telling you one thing; it is a refrain of which you are endlessly aware. Your heart tells you something quite different and you feel yourself betrayed.

In 1888 Katherine Mansfield is born in Wellington, New Zealand. At the age of fifteen she attends Queen's College, London. No doubt her father wishes her 'finished' in the manner of the time. In 1948 your mother comes to New Zealand, a woman of courage and sophistication, a devotee of Europe. Your father she meets in London, a New Zealand soldier convalescing from the war. They settle in the King Country, at a place so small its name is omitted from the road maps. Your mother likes the sound of 'the King Country', but soon finds that it is filled with dog bones and old wire.

She sends to Harrods for clothes to dress you, and your sisters when they come. You remember especially a white, large-wheeled pram. In high heels and stockings, she walks the pram across the farm. There are photographs to prove this. Look at you! Three little girls dressed all in white! There is lace, there are bows. There are little white socks. What will the kids think of you at school?

Your father is tall, a handsome man and rangy. All day the rams are tupping the ewes, despite the bidibids in their wool. On sale days your father roams the district, visiting other farmers' wives. The men wear oilskins and roll their own tobacco, are hoarse-voiced over bargains. In their absence your father is offered many cups of tea.

You marry a man who is taller and more handsome than your father. You don't know what else to do. During the birth of your son, your husband shouts at you for suffering. It is typical, he says, that you should make such a fuss about a little pain. When he marries a second time he calls his new son by the same name as your first. He cannot identify with imperfection; with this small, imperfect child. The lump when you discover it is just a marble in your breast. You tell your husband, but he will not discuss it. You find out later that he is having an affair. The doctor states it will have to go, that they will have to remove your breast.

The poet says she knows you when I interview her for the film. You sell the furniture and fly to California for a cure. This is ten years ago. Even then you like to travel. You discover that there are not enough apricot kernels in the whole wide world. The poet shows me passages in Katherine Mansfield's diaries, speaks of the 'great honesty' of her soul. Her poems are small domestic tragedies and she can write one every hour.

Today I prepare myself for the arrival of my new director, who is an upright man, and proud. I ask you to be his assistant because I can see you need the job. All morning I work on the scene of Katherine at Isola Bella; the writer is composing letters home; mimosa is heavy outside the casement and her room is full of light.

Over coffee we discuss your illness. There is a tumour in your chest that you insist on retaining to monitor the status of your disease. Throughout the history of your condition you witness tumours come and go. You are an international courier. The blood they give you in London is the blood that circulates in France.

Mme de Ferrier telephones and asks the three of us to lunch. You decide you do not like the banker, but accept charity for art.

You pause before the mirror but the mirror lets you pass. You are wearing your small black dress. You smile. You toss back glistening curls. The Mediterranean proceeds to Africa. Mimosa is close outside the window and light reflects its calm back to the world.

Stephanie Johnson

Stephanie Johnson (born 1961) is best known as a novelist, although she has worked as a playwright, scriptwriter and critic. She was Meridian Energy Katherine Mansfield Memorial Fellow in 2000, during which time she wrote, amongst other things, this poem which appeared in her 2003 collection, *Moody Bitch*.

Letter from Menton

I have my wish, it's raining and reminding me
of home. Two in the afternoon and from
the Alpes Maritimes clouds drop and break,
spread to stand without definition
monochrome over the sea, turning it black
as the back of a mirror. There's some wind
too, the first all summer, rubbing around
the heavy limbs of an old magnolia.

Eight letters in Auckland and four in rain:
eight for the city and half for its weather.
Sometimes in this cool room with door
open onto the garden—the camellias and palms—
I forget where I am.
I miss our time together, our long drifting
talk of work and books and how we make our way
through it all: our crowded, distracting lives.

The sun glares, turns the mirror over, the wind falls away.

Seagulls here have a Gaulish cry, loud
and somehow stylish. One sails now
over the railway line, his white back flaming.
He bends towards the stony coast. I'm thinking
of my uncertain return, of the meaning
of autonomy, duty and family and you, mon ami,
dans un autre monde et du tout ce je peux perdre,
all that I could lose.

224

Louis Johnson

Wellingtonian Louis Johnson (1924–88) published around 20 collections of verse during his life. His poems—often garrulous, opinionated ruminations on life, love and identity—are well represented in his *Selected Poems* (edited by Terry Sturm, 2000). Johnson died shortly after his tenure as Katherine Mansfield Memorial Fellow at Menton, during which time he wrote 'Côte d'Azur'.

Côte d'Azur

So many beautiful girls are wearing
the same face you'd swear they'd all bought masks
at a supermarket. I'm not complaining.

Beauty is beauty however processed
and regular. But when it becomes so uniform
something has got to give. Values diminish.

And I'm confused. I always knew there was
more to it than measurement, or that one year's
face would last a lifetime. Look at my own.

A walking, leering roadmap: and this morning
I limp along the waterfront on a cane from
falling downstairs to answer a late-night phone

and busting a leg on a radiator. But 1988
is the year the girls all look like peaches, their flesh
sweet and edible. They wear petulance

and a lisp as their trademarks. They parade
like fruit. I am glad to be old. I know if I must
choose again I'd do as badly as ever, and next

year, me and Miss Fourth-runner-up would be arguing
about who fooled who on a certain beach when
looking was free and all you had to decide was nothing.

Lauris Edmond

Lauris Edmond (1924–2000) received many awards for her poetry and was Katherine Mansfield Memorial Fellow in 1981. The following extract from her Menton diary can be found in the third volume of her autobiography, *The Quick World* (1992). These poems first appeared in *Catching It* (1983) and are included in her *Selected Poems*.

from **The Quick World**

March 29: 9.30pm I'm here! Not in the trying desert, not in dirty, beautiful, dangerous Damascus, not at Charles de Gaulle airport racing from desk to desk through that maze of miraculous constructions; not even in Nice where the little French bus waited while I struggled with my appalling luggage . . . Here. In Menton. In a safe, clean, courteous hotel—I don't care if it costs a million francs a night. And it's raining. Cool, soft, singing rain; I feel like a dying plant suddenly allowed to drink great gulps of fresh water.

There are enormous palm trees in the little square outside my window, tubs of primulas and cyclamen, a fountain. A man riding a bicycle has just bumped into a car; he fell off, but it was all very mild and moderate, acted in slow motion—the two navigators exchanged a few words, then both set off again (in Syria they would have shot each other). Everything already seems easy, wonderfully arranged after the chaotic and violent streets of Damascus, and the queer watchfulness in the hotel.

April 1: I'm more than ever here—right here, absolutely inside, living in the KM room. It's an elegant place; pale cream walls, aristocratic furniture, subtle lighting that flows magically out of panels high up on the walls; leaves across the windows—flax, good green New Zealand flax, at one, palm leaves like green fingers spread out at the other.

A small pebbled courtyard, a craggy tree (is it a loquat? I haven't seen one for years, but I think that's it), and the soft

226

pouf! pouf! of doves floating over the garden next door. It's all exactly right, and I am amazed and delighted that it is mine. There are daffodils in that garden too. I shall plant a red geranium in my corner plot, if I can find one.

But the getting here . . . I see myself standing helplessly in the Office de Tourisme while the briskest officials in the world plan my stay. They must find me a small cheap studio for six months; one of them begins ringing up. Alas no, the season will begin soon and who wants small cheap tenants then? They look at me despairingly. I could stay in the room, I murmur hesitantly. But why on earth hadn't I said so before? Oh, of course, no French. I am hurt by this and explain in their wretched language that I thought the mayors and councillors didn't approve of such an arrangement. Ach! It is sensible—a nice place—the best I could have—and so cheap, it will cost me nothing! Exactly, I think. I know there is no kitchen? I do, and expect to be able to manage.

Everything has become simple. We race off in the Mairie car to another office, collect the keys and another official who accompanies the driver and me to the room. There they carry my bags, switch on power and water, open everything, all in a moment. Then they lift up the corner of the bed cover—but I have no *draps*! They will return soon. They extract my mail from the locked letterbox, and vanish. I begin to read my letters, almost crying with relief and pleasure at finding that New Zealand did not after all drop off the end of the world, as in the Middle East it seemed perhaps it had.

In no time they are back with two enormous hem-stitched sheets, two satin-edged blankets, towels and a tubular pillow slip to cover the sausage body of my bolster. I cannot guess where it all came from (there are drycleaning tabs on the sheets—did they steal them?) but am grateful. We all shake hands. Then they remember something else, and out of the back of the car is drawn a tall, curly, polished wood umbrella stand. Since I have no real life-support system, no stove, bench, cupboard or refrigerator, not a cup or plate, knife or fork, this strikes me as a gloriously funny gesture. I smile broadly, we shake hands again and with manifold courtesies part at last.

How I luxuriate in being at home—my small, beautiful,

secret home for months and months. No doubt I shall be
lonely and unhappy, no doubt I shall wish for many things
I haven't got, but for the moment there is nothing, nothing,
nothing. There is no past and no future, only this island in
time, light as a bubble and shining with rainbow colours.

Easter Saturday in Menton

The afternoon's still; spring rain falls
straight, drenching wild roses that hang
their heads over this cracked stone wall.
Last night the people carried the wooden
body of Jesus black-wrapped through
the streets of the old town, singing
in high sad voices as they've done
for a thousand years; today they hang
crimson silk on the pillars of Saint
Michel for Christ risen on Easter Day.

The rich tourists are left to the cafés
or to elbow about in the gift shops
shouting they don't speak the local lingo.
I too am a stranger, not less for knowing
I shall read my own name on a locked
letter box in the next lane. I remember
Easter as gathering mushrooms in wet
paddocks, piling raw logs on the hearth,
in the sting of the smoke lighting
the first fires on autumn evenings.

The road is deserted; there are a few
shut iron gates in the hedges, eddies
of mud, rubbish tins—and the roses.
Their scent is sharp in the rain.

The Colour of Distance

Turning Point

All day I've been packing
and saying goodbye;
now I have just what I came with
—paper, a filled pen,
clothes for the journey.

The palm tree on the hill
turns and turns like a windmill
against the deepening sky
protesting that evening
has come too soon;

but further down the cypresses
are still, pointing as always
their dark fingers
and saying in shadowy voices
'Remember; remember.'

Lauris Edmond

Michael King

Before his untimely death in 2004, Michael King (born 1945) was New Zealand's leading biographer and historian. During his time as Katherine Mansfield Memorial Fellow in 1976, King completed the biography *Te Puea* (1977), as well as putting in some serious hours sailing on the Mediterranean. Over the past decade he published *Frank Sargeson* (1995), *Wrestling with the Angel: A Life of Janet Frame* (2000) and *The Penguin History of New Zealand* (2003).

Meeting Patrick White

For me, one of the unexpected joys of going to Menton was the opportunity it presented for meeting other writers. One such was Patrick White, who had been awarded the Nobel Prize for Literature three years earlier. The day I saw him peering through the windows of the Katherine Mansfield Room in Menton, tall, stooped, wearing a gabardine raincoat and beret, I concealed myself. I had had too many visitors in too short a period of time. When I read the card he slipped under the door, however, giving his name and inviting me to dinner, I relented. Who would not have?

Over several days, White and his companion, Manoly Lascaris, entertained me with great kindness. We went for walks on the beach, where Patrick professed to be disgusted by the number of women sunbathing topless ('Everything on display from ripe melons to dried figs!'). He gave me social advice over drinks: 'Of *course* the French don't invite you into their homes. You're a single man. They imagine you'd want to screw their wife and daughter. And if you didn't, they'd think there was something wrong with you. And when they *do* ask you, it's probably because they want you to . . .'

We went to the most expensive restaurant in town, where Madame de Gaulle (among others) was known to dine. The owner played the guitar and entertained guests with Provençal songs. Patrick, exaltedly inebriated, asked if she knew 'Knees Up Mother Brown'. When she shook her head, looking puzzled, he took the guitar from her and handed it to me. I played, and we three sang, 'Click Go the Shears', 'Waltzing Matilda' and 'The Pub With No Beer', which, Patrick explained to the now angry proprietor, were 'chansons ethnique du Sud Pacifique'.

White also got caught up in the kind of pomp and pomposity that he abhorred. The mayor's secretary, hearing that he was in town, asked me if he would attend a civic reception in his honour. It would, she said, help the municipality attract support for the KM Fellowship. White agreed, for that reason, but with the utmost reluctance. In the event, it was a fiasco. First, the mayor identified Lascaris as the guest of honour and ignored White. When that was resolved, he attempted to compensate for his blunder by making a long speech about how honoured Menton was to be dignified by a visit from as exalted a man as the eminent writer. The eminent writer glowered and began to drum his fingers audibly and ominously on the table. At the conclusion of these formalities, conducted entirely in French, the mayor's secretary asked Monsieur White if he required a translation. He did not. 'Actually,' said White, in a beautifully modulated voice, 'this sort of thing gives me the shits.' The mayor, imaging that he had been complimented, beamed and presented Patrick with several volumes of the *Transactions of the Menton Poetry Society*. They went into a council rubbish bin as we left the town hall soon after.

Michael Jackson

An anthropologist as well as a poet and novelist, Michael Jackson (born 1940) was Katherine Mansfield Memorial Fellow in 1982. During his Menton tenure he worked on the collection of poems *Going On* (1985), from which these poems are taken, and a novel, *Rainshadow* (1988). His collection of essays, *Pieces of Music* (1994), includes a memoir of Menton and a meditation on the French writer-aviator Antoine de Saint-Exupéry.

All Souls: Menton

Banks of white concrete
covered with chrysanthemums

On the Day of the Dead

The bread shops closed
and a ban on marriages

Row after row—
the English who died alone
in a villa in the sun,
women who survived
their husbands,
wreaths of porcelain.

Penitents hobble past
with bad legs or lungs
or simply lacking the will to live,
follow a clay track
to the paupers' ground
among cypresses.

These were the last to go—
who outlived a lineage
or got left behind

when their children migrated
from the coast—
who hoped at best a wooden cross
flowers from another grave

I envy them
claiming no room
on this expensive hill
paid for by the yard or year
to fake a memory

Go down
through the olive grove
to the room where I write

A gravel yard
five steps up
from an iron gate.

Villa Isola Bella

The muffled cor coro coo
of a ring-dove in the loquat tree

The morning sun spills out
like oranges on the sea

This musty room too long locked up
could be the room we had in Africa

Night after night I dream
of friends, their silences

I suffer all the traveller's maladies

I look into a blue haze

Michael Jackson   233

Elizabeth Knox

Elizabeth Knox set her 2004 novel *Daylight* around the Franco-Italian border and along the coast from Marseilles to Genoa. A vampire novel, *Daylight* features vividly-realised settings such as the Palais Lutetia in Menton, which has housed Katherine Mansfield Memorial Fellows since 1991.

from **Daylight**

Eve heard Ila and Dawn arrive at the Menton apartment in the early hours of the morning. She thought she heard her sister laughing and wondered what Ila—silent Ila—might have done to make Dawn laugh.

After breakfast Eve went out to Martine's funeral—at which she was the sole mourner, Father Octave having failed to appear. She followed her friend up to the Moskelute tomb, oversaw the interment, and received its key from the undertaker. Eve thanked him and the priest and pallbearers. She pocketed the key and walked down through the old town.

She didn't go back to the apartment but spent the rest of the day in a manner customary to other Mentonnais of her station. She went to a patisserie and had a pear tart and a coffee. She sat in the shade on a park bench, beneath the orange trees on the Avenue Verdun. She nodded or spoke briefly to people she knew and once went into a café to borrow an ashtray, into which she poured some mineral water to rehydrate a tiny white-haired troll of a dog who had been left tethered to the leg of a bench by its master, who was asleep but plugged into a radio giving a running commentary on a bicycle race.

Eve was too late for the markets, so she went into a shop opposite the entrance to her street, bought several overripe tomatoes, a baguette, and a cylinder of soft goat's cheese coated with ash. She took her time considering wine—since she was choosing for Dawn and Ila as well as for herself.

When she left the shop she stood still for a moment, dazzled by reflections, the low, angled sunlight on the glossy patches of old chewing gum plastered to the pavement, then set off across the delta of roadway at the bus station. At the entrance to the steep street to her apartment block Eve paused to let a car go by. It was a long car and swung out in order to make the turn into the narrow entry. Its windows were mirrored, and Eve saw herself in its beetle green glass, foreshortened and as pale as a wraith. The car revved and ran up the hill.

Eve went slowly, stopping now and then to catch her breath. She trudged up the Palais Lutetia's front steps. It had rained in Menton while she was up in the Roya Valley, for the recently trimmed red and purple bougainvillea on the balustrade had sprouted fresh, questing shoots. Eve waited a moment in the sun, panting and hitching her shoulders to free the fabric of her shirt from the patch of sweat on her back. She noticed the car that had passed her, stopped in the yellow-painted turning space of the *palais*'s inadequate parking lot. Its driver was still sitting in it. Eve had the impression he was watching her. She squinted but couldn't penetrate the reflective glass to see who he might be.

Eve pushed herself up the steps and went into her building.

It was cooler in the lobby beneath the apartment's central well, where stairs with marble treads wound up ten floors around an elevator shaft fenced with bronze mesh. The Moskelute apartment was on the second floor, but because it was her habit when burdened by shopping, Eve went to the elevator. As she put her hand into the handle of its concertinaed door, Eve heard footfalls behind her. Someone was hurrying up the flight of steps from the outer door to the entrance hall. Eve glanced back over her shoulder and saw a shapeless shadow against the blue late-afternoon sky and the orange-tiled roofs of the apartments down the slope. The figure came into the light from the stairwell and Eve saw his enveloping coat, ski mask, shades, gloved hands.

She hauled the elevator door open and lunged inside. The elevator cage shook. She swept the outer door closed and heard its catch click. She slid the inner door into place and flung herself away from the hand that snaked through the two cages and made a grab at her. She hit the up button.

The elevator hummed and began to move. Eve backed against the cage's far wall. As the elevator went up, she stooped to keep her attacker in sight.

The figure moved swiftly. Eve could suddenly see the whole rectangle of light from the front door. She began to jab as many buttons as she could and, as she'd hoped, the Palais Lutetia's aged and temperamental elevator came to a stubborn stop. Eve looked up and saw boots, the swinging hem of a long coat. He was on the second floor before the elevator and at the call button. She heard the button rattle as he pressed it rapidly, over and over.

The elevator didn't move.

The wrapped figure crept slowly back down.

Sunlight came through the tall windows that gave a view from each of the *palais*'s landings through the rear of the building and back toward the east, where the sun was touching the top of the high barrier of the Maritime Alps. There was a patch of hard, hot late-afternoon sun on the first marble-tiled landing. The bundled figure edged past it, his masked and hooded head averted. He came back down the lower flight. He stopped in the hall, raised his head, and looked into the elevator cage at Eve. He seized the outer cage and shook it.

A booming echoed up and down the height of the building. The metal grated and complained.

Michael King

from **Wrestling with the Angel:**
A Life of Janet Frame

One reason for falling asleep on that first visit to the 'stone chamber' was that Frame had arrived in Menton with influenza. She spent the first week based at the Villa Louise, a pension next door to Isola Bella, which she described as 'so *fin de siècle* that I feel as if I'm living in a film or fiction. The guests grow more & more to resemble the marble of the staircases . . . The meals are tremendous & go on & on—if you saw the film *Death in Venice* you'd get the setting.' A literary pilgrim from Paris who shared Frame's table at the pension gave her a glimpse of how highly Mansfield was revered by her French readers. This woman came to Menton every year on the anniversary of the writer's death (9 January). When Frame suffered a fit of coughing, a consequence of her flu, this woman said to her, 'Have you read the journal of Katherine Mansfield? She was from New Zealand and had a cough like yours.'

Frame *did* read Mansfield's journal that week, in French, 'and found it so much more moving . . . than in English . . . [I feel] more admiration for her now. She really was an exile . . . and all her happiest dreams were of Wellington; whereas I, when I have nightmares, they are always of New Zealand.'

Also in Menton at the time of Frame's arrival were two of the fellowship's major New Zealand patrons, Cecil and Celia Manson, and their thirty-year-old son, Bill. They advanced her money to compensate for the non-appearance of the stipend, and wined and dined her in some of the town's best restaurants. Cecil looked like 'a faded English colonel. I get on very well with him & I'm moved by his obvious devotion to his son & his pride in him; & the son is so gentle & sympathetic to his parents, in spite of his embarrassment at their pride. The mother is very intelligent & slightly bewildered, with a powdered face.' In café conversation with Bill and his partner, Carlita Foss, Frame pointed to a young man passing in the street and said, 'If I'd had a son that could be him.' They misunderstood her to say that she *had* a son of that age, which led subsequently to a rumour to that effect in New Zealand; and to at least one rosy-cheeked, red haired man claiming to be that son.

The other favour the Mansons performed was to help establish Frame in what they hoped would be her permanent accommodation in the town, a tiny one-room apartment in Garavan, which would cost six hundred francs a month, half her stipend. Her initial plan was to work in the memorial room and to eat and sleep in the bed-sitter. The next problem, however, was that the typewriter which had been left in the room by the first fellow, Owen Leeming, was now 'battered and useless . . . the legs go down and won't go up'. Continental typewriters would be no substitute, because the keyboard placings were different from those on an 'English' typewriter. Eventually, however, she found a second-hand model that was satisfactory.

In the third week in January, shortly after the Mansons had left and before she had been able to settle to work, Frame was sought out and 'rescued' by another New Zealand writer, Anton Vogt, who was temporarily resident in Menton. Vogt, as he liked to tell anyone who was listening, had been conceived in the Argentine, born in Norway, and educated in England, Switzerland and South Africa. He had come to New Zealand with his family in his early teens and developed there into a poet, gifted teacher and controversialist. It was he who had put John Money in touch with Denis Glover in 1946 to arrange publication of Frame's first book; and he had been one of the judges who awarded her the Hubert Church prize in 1952. Vogt too had featured with Frame in the first Oxford University Press anthology of New Zealand stories, and he had written to the *New Zealand Listener* in defence of *Owls Do Cry* when that novel was given a less than wholly enthusiastic review. He was in Menton in 1974 on sabbatical leave from Simon Fraser University in Vancouver. He and his wife, Birgitte, had bought and were redecorating two houses there, one to live in after his retirement and the other to rent out for income.

When they found Frame, both Vogts were appalled by the state of the memorial room ('It's degrading [for] Janet Frame to work there'); and by the claustrophobic and expensive nature of her accommodation. In the last week in January 1974 they invited her to live in their rental property, a green-shuttered cottage alongside their own house in Avenue Cernuschi, about twenty minutes' walk from Garavan.

Frame was delighted to accept. 'There's no suggestion of squalor as there was inclined to be in the other place. Everything is new and fresh and Birgitte has put all the housewifely touches to it . . . I have my own yard and table-in-the-sun, and my own two storeys in the house . . . My bedroom is downstairs, with lavatory, shower and two washbasins . . . while upstairs is the big sitting-room looking out over Italy with two divans, a kitchen . . . and a bathroom with [a] huge bath . . . [It] is right in Menton, but in a *cul de sac*, literally an oasis, with all the palm trees.' All this would cost her no more than she had previously paid for the single room.

Frame was also delighted by the Vogts' company. They brought her to their house for occasional lunches and dinners; and she reciprocated. They also took her on periodic outings in their open-topped sports car—across the Italian border to Ventimiglia, up to mountain villages in the Alpes Maritimes, to places of cultural and historical interest such as Eze, La Turbie, and Roquebrun, where W. B. Yeats had died in 1939. 'They [are] careful to respect my privacy and I . . . theirs. It's just the kind of good fortune that I seem to have from time to time,' she told Bill Brown. There were also echoes of Oamaru, albeit exotic ones.

[Yesterday] I went exploring . . . up the back of the Vogts' land where they have never been yet, and I was so pleased to come back with an armful of wild freesias. It's really lovely up there—big pine trees, mimosas, a eucalyptus, and a wild growth of little olive trees and broom, and grass to lie in and really feel alone in the world; and far out is the sea, and the coast of Italy. I know where to find some peace and aloneness—it's very much the feeling of being a child again and (as the womb is locked and chained) finding a secret place in the grass.

By mid-February Frame was contentedly settled and beginning to work—in the cottage, not the memorial room. 'After writing six short stories I have finally (cross fingers and hearts) begun a novel which I have planned to finish . . . about the end of June.' She was trying out what she called her 'adventures' in the French language on shopkeepers, and on the family of Bernard Tardy, the town's genial and handsome director of tourism, who was responsible for local administration of the Katherine Mansfield Fellowship. '[Although] my conversation is pretty awful, when I read French I have a feeling as if I'm doing it from the "inside" with it surrounding me like a kind of lining, whereas before I was "outside" and had to tear the material to get in.' She also wrote a considerable number of poems in French, including one for the Tardys' ten-year-old son, Etienne, which read in part:

Etienne, Etienne.
Il a dix ans.
Il pique comme les abeilles qui'il attrappe.
Etienne, Etienne.
C'est certain qu'il est sur le Massif Central,
Etienne, la turbie, la bise, le mistral,
et les abeilles mortes, suffoquées,
qui faisent, il était une fois,
le miel de jasmin.

Frame never ceased to be charmed by the character of Menton and its environs. 'It has rained for days now, with a heavy low grey sky and no wind and the mountains—the tail end of the Alps—seen from here are wonderfully mysterious, wrapped in mist . . . Anton and Birgitte asked me if I would like to . . . visit Ste-Agnès, the highest mountain village on the coast. So [we] went on a very pleasant excursion [and] talked to an old man who is 115 . . . He was sitting on a stone seat, out in the cold, with the snow on the mountains above him, and he wore a bright blue nylon raincoat. He was blind.'

Other Menton residents offered her hospitality, including a retired English Member of Parliament, John Martin, who had been a friend of John Middleton Murry at Oxford, and his wife, Dorothy. 'He is quite old [in his eighties], she a little younger ... [Their] apartment is overrun with books—Virginia Woolf lying beside D. H. Lawrence on the coffee table! They pressed books upon me . . . and I came home with Keats' Letters, some of Somerset Maugham's stories, French poetry and Proust in French . . . Longtemps je me suis couchée de bonne heure . . . What a lovely beginning.'

Late in February John Money came to stay for a few days after attending a conference in Geneva. He shared both Frame's delight in the Côte d'Azur and the Vogts' indignation at what seemed to be the poor administration of the fellowship (Frame had received only her first month's stipend payment from Wellington) and the condition of the memorial room. As soon as he was back in Baltimore he fired off a letter to the *New Zealand Listener*. The Katherine Mansfield Room, he pointed out, had neither 'water, gas nor electricity. It is furnished with a portable burner for heating, a small table, chair and portable typewriter, and a kerosene lamp. The lamp is needed even at midday, as the small apertured window does not permit sufficient illumination, and the climate does not always permit the door to be kept open. There are no toilet facilities . . . [Made] aware of these conditions, New Zealanders will, I hope, in haste do something to correct them.'

To complement this letter, Anton Vogt wrote a feature for the *Listener* in which he elaborated on Money's description of the room and added historical background. He also commented: 'Few New Zealand writers would expect to live in the luxury to which Katherine Mansfield was accustomed . . . Nevertheless, some things can be done to make a fellowship in her honour an honour . . . One is not to ask any writer to occupy the cell. Another is to provide a living wage of not less than 2000 francs per month . . . A third might well be to forget the romantic allegiance to Isola Bella, except as a mausoleum; and to buy a small apartment or flat nearby for perhaps 100,000 francs, to be available rent-free to subsequent Fellows.'

In reply, Karl Stead referred to Vogt's piece as an 'extravagant overstatement' of the shortcomings of the room and the fellowship, and accused him of 'selective malice . . . [In] view of the fact that renovations are planned and money promised for them [by the municipality of Menton], his attack—which amounts to an attack on the Fellowship—seems quite pointless.' Cecil and Celia Manson also responded, pointing out that the state of the room was the responsibility of the authorities in Menton, not the New Zealand fellowship committee. Embarrassingly for Frame, they quoted her as saying, when they had told her about the promised renovations, 'Oh, what a pity! I love the room as it is.'

By this time, May 1974, Frame was close to abandoning the fellowship. Not because of the state of the room, but because her payments from Wellington were still overdue; and the organising committee was not replying to her requests for the remission of the whole stipend, nor to her queries about whether she was permitted to fly home via the United States. Eventually the rest of the money did arrive, four months late. 'But,' said Frame, 'they'll never know how much I have been put off my work, waiting.' As for the published opinions about the state of the memorial room, Frame pronounced them all to be 'equally truthful . . . If I'd been a ghost with no bodily functions and no need of light, I'd happily have made the room my headquarters. I'm pleased [to hear] that future Fellows may have the advantage of . . . improvements.' The public airing of criticism produced a salutary result. The French Embassy in Wellington put pressure on the Menton municipality to carry out its undertaking to upgrade the memorial room and to install a bathroom. Work on these alterations had begun before Frame left Menton in August 1974.*

* There was a side-bar to this controversy. Frank Sargeson wrote to a friend that he was 'much troubled by the Vogt–Money stuff in the *Listener* . . . I feel I may be lucky to have escaped criticism for the sort of place [my] hut was to inhabit.'

Bill Manhire

Villa Ephrussi

Cap-Ferrat, 1911

1.
Béatrice Ephrussi waits at the station at Beaulieu,
while the ancient world arrives by train.

Stone and marble and canvas are laid out before her,
everything there on the platform.

Wife of a banker, daughter of a banker.

This, she says.
                 And *this* and *this*.
Also those chairs.

And that—what is it?—*pediment*,
perhaps it might go to the lapidary garden.

As for the rest, send them away.

*

She is so busy!

Pink house, blue sea, green garden.
It is hard when you must do everything yourself.

She buys a ruined chapel
and simply removes the fresco.
The rest can go . . . somewhere . . .

she doesn't know where . . . perhaps
once again the *jardin lapidaire*

with its superfluous gods and heroes,
busts and columns and so on,
all of the clutter and overflow

from a house composed of attributions:
suite and drawing room
and drawing room and wealth

and dining room and suite and patio
with those pink marble colonnades from Verona—
ah Tiepolo, Lancret, Carpaccio—

and 30 servants at work indoors,
with 30 more out in the garden
wearing their red berets, all dressed as sailors.

At night they haul on ropes
and the great garden sails out,
heading towards Africa . . .

2.
Oh, all of the gardens of the world are here!

Spanish and Japanese and Florentine,
the Rosery where everything is pink,
'in fragrant profusion',
the Provençal, the Exotic

and of course the French—
formal and clipped
and there at the centre.

*

Yet always so busy! When can she rest?
Perhaps for a moment, yes now for a moment,
at her 'Happiness of the Day' writing desk . . .

for tonight she keeps company
with music and with light . . .

Guests are gathering around the fountain
and soon she will dress as Marie-Antoinette

and descend through polite applause
to enter a hundred conversations.

3.
She married a banker, the Baron Ephrussi
—a man of wealth like her father—
though he also traded in grain.

But it can't have been only the money.
She was a Rothschild, you see,
so that was no problem.

No, there was a chemistry between them,
there was what they say in books.
When he lit her cigarette, see how the flame trembled!

And yet, poor Béatrice.

The villa was finished in 1912,
and only four years later 'Frousse', as she called him,
deleting both ends of the surname,

Frousse, her husband Maurice, died.

Now she was really at sea.
In fact, she was terrified: *avoir la frousse*,
the French say, which means

to be in a funk, to have the wind up, to have the jitters.

Bill Manhire   245

She closed up the house forever.
It had been a love nest, you see.
Vast, but a love nest.

It was the end of 'an unforgettable journey'.

4.
Yes, always the wonderful days are gone.
There is proper wealth, and some people have it,
then eventually the crooks, the *crapules*, take over.

You hear people talking like this.

What would she think, Béatrice,
now that her whole coast is made of boats
and all of her gardens fill with brides?

One by one, they arrive on the hour,
cream and ivory and lace,
each with a groom, of course,
and a white-shirted photographer.

From the *salon de thé*,
where wine is sold by the glass,
we watch them searching for backgrounds.

A shot in the Spanish Garden, next to the dolphin,
(but not the exotic cacti, with their terrifying spikes),

and one between bamboo and temple
or beside the snow-viewing lantern . . .

and finally—of course!—
the bride shining alone in front of the fountain

while the groom smokes a cigarette
and stares down at the carpark . . .

The Colour of Distance